GREAT PLANTS
For GEORGIA GARDENS
50

FLOWERS
GEORGIA
for

FLOWERS
GEORGIA *for*

Erica Glasener
Walter Reeves

COOL
SPRINGS
PRESS

Nashville, Tennessee
A Division of Thomas Nelson, Inc.
www.ThomasNelson.com

Published by Cool Springs Press, a Division of Thomas Nelson, Inc.
P.O. Box 141000, Nashville, Tennessee, 37214.

First printing 2004
Printed in the United States of America
10 9 8 7 6 5 4 3 2 1

Managing Editor: Mary Morgan
Horticulture Editor: Michael Wenzel, Atlanta Botanical Garden
Copyeditor: Michelle Adkerson
Designer: Bill Kersey, Kersey Graphics
Production Artist: S.E. Anderson

On the cover: Japanese Roof Iris, photographed by Jerry Pavia

We gratefully acknowledge the contribution of the following author who has granted her permission to use selected entries:

Globe Amaranth (pg. 52), New Guinea Impatiens (pg. 76), and Pentas (pg. 80)—Judy Lowe

Visit the Thomas Nelson website at www.ThomasNelson.com

Table *of* Contents

How To Use This Book

Each entry in this guide provides you with information about a plant's particular characteristics, habits, and basic requirements for active growth as well as our personal experience and knowledge of the plant. We include the information you need to help you realize each plant's potential. Only when a plant performs at its best can one appreciate it fully. You will find such pertinent information as mature height and spread, bloom period and colors, sun and soil preferences, water requirements, fertilizing needs, pruning and care, and pest information.

Sun Preferences

Symbols represent the range of sunlight suitable for each plant. Some plants can be grown in more than one range of sun, so you will sometimes see more than one sun symbol.

Full Sun　　**Part Sun/Shade**　　**Full Shade**

Additional Benefits

Many plants offer benefits that further enhance their appeal. The following symbols indicate some of the more important additional benefits:

 Attracts Butterflies

 Attracts Hummingbirds

 Produces Edible Fruit

 Has Fragrance

 Produces Food for Birds and Wildlife

 Drought Resistant

 Suitable for Cut Flowers or Arrangements

 Long Bloom Period

 Native Plant

 Supports Bees

 Good Fall Color

 Provides Shelter for Birds

Complementary Plants

For many of the entries, we provide landscape design ideas as well as suggestions for companion plants to help you achieve striking and personal gardening results from your garden. This is where we find the most enjoyment from gardening.

Recommended Selections

This section describes specific cultivars or varieties that are particularly noteworthy. Give them a try.

50 Great Flowers *for* Georgia

Flowers are the jewels of the landscape and are what most people think of first when they think of gardening. With their wide variety of shapes, colors, textures, fragrance, even life cycles, flowers offer endless opportunities to create appealing combinations that delight all the senses. We are fortunate in Georgia to be able to grow many different types of flowers. In many ways we live in a plant paradise. We have a very long growing season, with mild, short winters and abundant sunshine, so we can grow both perennials that need a cold dormant season and plants that won't survive our winters but love the heat and get enough of it here to put on a show for months. By combining these two types of flowers, our gardens can be gorgeous from February through November.

Coleus

Life Cycles of Flowers

In this book, we refer to flowers as either annuals or perennials. Technically, annuals are plants that grow, set seed, and die in one season, although we also use the term for any plant that will not survive our winters outdoors. Perennials are plants that live at least several years, and sometimes many years, with their foliage dying away and disappearing over winter, then sprouting again in spring. Tropical plants, such as impatiens, are treated as annuals in Georgia, although they are perennial in climates such as south Florida's. And some annuals—cosmos come to mind—self-seed, meaning they scatter their seeds around so new plants appear season after season.

It isn't necessary to know exactly which horticultural category a flower falls into in order to enjoy it and succeed with it. The important things you need to know are whether the plant will winter over or not and how long it will stay in bloom. Annuals and most tropicals bloom from spring to frost, while perennials stay in bloom only a few weeks. Many perennials have very attractive foliage, though, and can play useful roles in the garden even when not in bloom.

Selecting Flowers

When selecting flowers for your garden, consider several factors:

Planting conditions. Check the light, soil, and water conditions where you plan to plant. Most annuals are sun lovers. If you have many trees in your yard, look for flowers that prefer shade. Only a few plants will grow in poor soil, so work up your soil to about a foot deep, add organic matter (such as finely shredded bark, rotted leaves, rotted manure, or compost), and work it in thoroughly. Remove all grass and weeds, including roots, before working the soil.

Color. Choose colors that coordinate with your house and with other plantings in the yard. Some gardeners prefer all one color while others enjoy combining colors. White and light colors are especially nice where you can see them in the evening—around the deck or patio, for example.

Mature height. Flowers come in heights from a few inches to several feet, although most annuals grow to about a foot tall. You want a combination of heights, so look for plants that vary. In general, it's best to put lower growing plants at the front of the garden, with mid-sized plants behind and tall ones at the back.

Gaillardia

Pentas

Culture Basics

Devoting time in the beginning to do a really good job of improving your soil and removing weeds pays off huge dividends down the road. Beyond that, flowers need water, fertilizer, deadheading (picking off the blossoms that are past their prime in order to keep the plant from putting energy into producing seeds) unless you want the plant to self-seed, and a careful eye for disease or insect problems.

Since annuals bloom heavily for so long, they need more fertilizer than perennials do. Overfertilizing perennials can cause them to become weak and floppy. If you've done a good job adding organic matter to your soil, perennials need little if any added fertilizer. If you're mixing annuals and perennials together, one way to handle their different needs is to use a slow-release fertilizer in the planting holes for annuals or, if you enjoy fertilizing, to sprinkle them every few weeks with a water-soluble fertilizer.

Watering and weeding are essential for all flowers. Plants need about 1 inch of water per week, so use your rain gauge to tell you when to water. And do so thoroughly and deeply, all at one time, rather than sprinkling lightly every day. Deep watering encourages deep roots, making the plants more drought resistant.

11

Alumroot

Heuchera micrantha 'Palace Purple' and *Heuchera americana*

A Perennial with Foliage So Gorgeous That the Flowers Are a Bonus

It's the evergreen foliage of alumroot that steals the show, not its flowers, though those are dainty and loved by hummingbirds. *Heuchera americana* has marbled leaves in combinations of green with silver or white. *H. micrantha* 'Palace Purple' has purple-bronze foliage. Both provide instant and long-season color in the flower garden or at the edge of a woodland. The foliage of these two alumroots stands out when other perennials are looking tired and faded.

Top Reasons to Plant

- Beautiful foliage in varied color combinations
- Delicate sprays of colorful blooms
- Attracts hummingbirds
- Good cut flower
- Prefers shade
- Excellent planted near paths and patios where the foliage can be seen
- Few pests or diseases
- Likes moist situations

Useful Hint

Heuchera americana makes a good ground cover and tolerates fairly dry soils in sun or shade.

Bloom Color
White, pink, or red

Bloom Period
April to August depending on variety

Height/Width
12 to 24 inches x 12 to 18 inches

Planting Location
- Moist, well-drained soil, with compost or other organic matter added
- Shade or partial shade

Planting
- Set out in spring or fall.
- Space plants 8 to 12 inches apart.
- Water well after planting.
- Mulch well.

Watering
- Keep soil moist but never saturated.

Fertilizing
- Fertilize in early spring with half an inch of compost or a pelleted, slow-release plant food at *half* the amount recommended on the label.

Suggestions for Vigorous Growth
- Cut faded flowers with their stems to keep plants neat and to encourage reblooming.
- Renew mulch each year.
- Divide clumps in early spring every third year and replant immediately.
- When dividing, take care to break the plant apart rather than cut through the crown.

Easy Tip
Try cutting a few leaves from established heucheras to use in flower arrangements.

- If older plants develop woody stems and sprawl about, dig them up, remove the oldest part, and replant a little deeper.

Pest Control
- Heucheras have few insect or disease problems.

Complementary Plants
- Plant with foamflower, ferns, crested iris, liriope, and blue-leaved hostas.

Recommended Selections
- 'Garnet' has garnet foliage in spring and winter.
- 'Pewter Veil' has copper-pink leaves in spring that fade to a metallic color with purple undersides as the summer progresses.
- 'Palace Purple' has ivy-shaped leaves that start out purple-bronze in spring, then become more green with the heat of summer.

Arkansas Blue Star
Amsonia hubrichtii

A Heat-Loving Perennial with Delicate Flowers and Handsome Foliage

Because blooms are often "here today and gone tomorrow," it's important to consider foliage when choosing perennials for our Georgia gardens. One gem is the little-known *Amsonia hubrichtii*, which offers delicate, blue, star-shaped flowers in late spring and handsome foliage throughout the growing season. The leaves whorl around the stem, giving the effect of a small willow. In fall, the delicate leaves turn golden-yellow.

Top Reasons to Plant

○ Showy spring flowers
○ Lovely fall color
○ Tolerates variety of soils
○ Attractive foliage texture
○ Needs little care
○ Few pests and diseases

Useful Hint

Arkansas blue star's fine texture provides a good contrast for plants such as chrysanthemum, iris, black-eyed Susan, purple coneflower, bee balm, and some of the more sun-tolerant hostas, such as 'Sum and Substance'.

Bloom Color
Pale sky-blue

Bloom Period
Late spring

Height/Width
2¹/₂ to 3 feet x 2¹/₂ to 3 feet

Planting Location
- Prefers slightly acidic, moist, well-drained soil with lots of organic matter but adapts to a wide range of soils
- Sun or light shade

Planting
- Set out plants in early spring or fall.
- Space plants 2 feet apart.
- Dig the hole two to three times larger than the plant's container.
- Set the plant at the same depth as it was growing in the container.
- Water well.

Watering
- Water deeply during periods of drought.

Fertilizing
- No fertilizer is needed.

Suggestions for Vigorous Growth
- If the plant becomes leggy after blooming, cut it back to keep it bushy.
- You need not divide clumps, but if you wish to, divide in early spring or fall—plant divisions immediately and water them well.

Easy Tip
In just a few years, Arkansas blue star forms a large clump as wide as it is high, so give it plenty of room.

Pest Control
- Few insects or diseases trouble this plant.

Complementary Plants
- For a dramatic effect, plant Arkansas blue star in groups to present masses of finely textured foliage.
- Plant with other spring-blooming perennials.
- Use with fall-blooming asters for a nice show—Arkansas blue star's foliage colors beautifully about the time asters bloom.

Recommended Selections
- Though *Amsonia tabernaemontana* is better known and slightly more cold hardy, the leaves are much wider and the effect isn't the same—if you have room for only one blue star, plant *Amsonia hubrichtii*.

Artemisia

Artemisia 'Powis Castle'

A Perennial with Outstanding, Lacy, Silvery-Gray Foliage

'Powis Castle' can sometimes be too successful, taking over other plants. Placed in the right location, its finely textured, silvery-gray foliage offers interest year-round. But one word of caution: 'Powis Castle' can grow to the size of a small car in just a few seasons. Though you can cut it back, for best results, propagate it from cuttings every two or three years, and replant it.

Top Reasons to Plant

- ○ Beautiful silvery-gray foliage with fine texture
- ○ Tolerates drought
- ○ Easy care
- ○ Shows off other, more colorful plants
- ○ Softens the look of the garden
- ○ Useful for flower arrangements
- ○ Good filler in the garden

Useful Hint

Produce more plants by rooting the cuttings you pinch off in a mixture of 1 part sand to 1 part potting soil.

Bloom Color
Grown for lace-cut, silvery-gray leaves

Bloom Period
Foliage effective from summer to fall

Height/Width
2 to 3 feet x 3 feet

Planting Location
- Well-drained soil
- Full sun, but withstands some afternoon shade

Planting
- Set out purchased plants or rooted cuttings in spring.
- Add organic matter or sand to the soil to ensure good drainage.
- Water well after planting.
- Mulch lightly.

Watering
- Once established, 'Powis Castle' shouldn't need watering except during periods of drought.

Fertilizing
- No fertilizer is required.

Suggestions for Vigorous Growth
- Prune 'Powis Castle' in late spring if it gets leggy and open.
- Any cutting back should be done no earlier than early spring just before new growth begins or no later than early summer to allow the plant to recover before winter.
- Pinch the growing tips of the plant throughout the season to keep 'Powis Castle' compact.
- Do not overwater.

Easy Tip
Artemisia may suffer during wet weather, but it is quick to recover as long as the soil doesn't remain wet.

Pest Control
- Yellow spots on the lower leaves indicate rust, a fungal disease that can develop in humid conditions.
- If rust develops, cut the plant back to the ground, removing all leaves from the garden and destroying them.

Complementary Plants
- 'Powis Castle' is an excellent filler plant with antique or English roses, purple coneflowers, salvias, and chrysanthemums.

Recommended Selections
- 'Powis Castle' has proved to be one of the best for our hot, humid summers, but it is probably not suited for coastal gardens.

Bath's Pink

Dianthus gratianopolitanus 'Bath's Pink'

A Perennial with Spicy Fragrance and Lots of Charm

This delightful dianthus, or pink, was discovered in Georgia by Jane Bath of Stone Mountain. It was named in her honor by the owners of Goodness Grows, a wonderful nursery in Lexington, Georgia, that specializes in perennials. In early spring, usually April, masses of clove-scented, pink, fringed flowers create a blanket of bloom atop mounds of blue-gray, needlelike foliage. This fast spreader forms a tightly woven carpet that looks good all year.

Top Reasons to Plant

○ Lovely spring flowers
○ Fragrant
○ Attractive blue-gray foliage
○ Spreads quickly
○ Withstands summer heat

Useful Hint

If you're concerned about drainage, plant 'Bath's Pink' a little higher than it was growing previously.

Bloom Color
Soft pink

Bloom Period
April and May

Height/Width
9 to 12 inches x 9 to 12 inches

Planting Location
- Well-drained, moderately fertile soil
- Sun

Planting
- Set out plants in early spring or fall.
- Dig the hole as large as the plant's container.
- Set the plant at the same level it was growing previously.
- Firm the soil around the rootball.
- Water well.

Watering
- Once the plant becomes well established, water only during periods of drought.

Fertilizing
- No fertilizer is needed.

Suggestions for Vigorous Growth
- Remove spent flowers before they set seed.
- After bloom is completed, shear plants back to tidy mounds.
- Divide clumps every two or three years, when they begin opening up in the middle.

Easy Tip
Cuttings taken in early summer are very easy to root in wet sand to increase your number of plants.

Pest Control
- No serious pests or diseases trouble this plant.

Complementary Plants
- For an excellent effect, use as edging in front of a flower border or as ground cover creeping over a wall or in a rock garden.
- Plant as a "weaver" to fill in gaps between perennials in a border.
- Combine with early tulips that bloom at the same time as Bath's pink.

Recommended Selections
- 'Bath's Pink' may be the perfect perennial for Georgia gardens.
- *Dianthus* 'Itsaul White' is a fragrant white-flowered selection.

Bee Balm

Monarda didyma

A Spreading Perennial with Showy Blooms

Bee balm is a mint relative, as you'll know when you brush against a leaf and smell the aroma. Quick to spread, especially in shady places, this native can be invasive, which makes it ideal for naturalizing in a meadow or along a stream. With its square stems and large flower heads, it's much beloved by bees and hummingbirds during its blooming season. Also called bergamot, the leaves are a key ingredient of Earl Grey tea.

Top Reasons to Plant

○ Showy flowers
○ Attracts bees, butterflies, and hummingbirds
○ Tough and hardy
○ Adapts to various conditions
○ Good cut flower
○ Decorative seedheads

Useful Hint

Moist soils with some shade and good air circulation help reduce the chance of powdery mildew on bee balm.

Bloom Color
Scarlet, red, pink, violet, or white

Bloom Period
Summer

Height/Width
2 to 4 feet x 2 to 4 feet

Planting Location
• Moist, well-drained, fertile soil
• Good air circulation
• Sun, partial shade, or shade

Planting
• Set out plants in early spring.
• Space plants 18 to 24 inches apart.
• Water well.
• Mulch heavily.

Watering
• Keep plants watered during periods of drought.

Fertilizing
• No fertilizer is needed.

Suggestions for Vigorous Growth
• Deadheading prolongs the blooming period, but the dry seedheads add ornamental interest to the garden.
• Divide plants every three years to keep them from taking over the garden.

Easy Tip
The dried seedheads of bee balm are good for decorative arrangements indoors.

Pest Control
• Powdery mildew may be a problem— if foliage gets covered, shear plants back in late summer for a new flush of growth.

Complementary Plants
• Use to excellent effect in naturalized areas.
• Combine with other summer-blooming perennials in the flower garden.
• Plant along the edge of a woodland garden next to hostas.

Recommended Selections
• 'Jacob Cline' is a cultivar with intense red flowers.
• 'Croftway Pink' has pink flowers all summer.
• 'Cambridge Scarlet' grows 4 to 5 feet tall and has scarlet-red flowers.

Bigroot Geranium
Geranium macrorrhizum

A Heat-Loving Perennial That's a Wonderful Ground Cover

True geraniums are a diverse group of hardy perennials in the genus *Geranium*—don't confuse them with the common container plant geranium, which is in the genus *Pelargonium* and comes in colors from electric-red to shocking-pink. Of the perennial geraniums, bigroot is one of the easiest to grow. It holds up well in our summer heat even during drought, and its vigorous roots spread quickly, making a dense ground cover few weeds can penetrate.

Top Reasons to Plant

- Attractive flowers
- Spreads quickly
- Few insect or disease problems
- Thrives in shade
- Drought tolerant
- Smothers weeds

Useful Hint

Hardy geraniums are little-known, versatile perennials many gardeners haven't yet discovered—their flowers come in a range of colors, with foliage that varies in texture from delicate to coarse.

Bloom Color
Magenta, white, or pink

Bloom Period
Spring

Height/Width
15 to 18 inches x 18 to 24 inches

Planting Location
- Moist, well-drained soil containing lots of organic matter
- Partial sun or shade

Planting
- Set plants out in early spring or fall.
- Space plants 18 to 24 inches apart.
- Water well.
- Mulch heavily.

Watering
- Provide an inch of water in weeks without that amount of rainfall.

Fertilizing
- Topdress with organic matter once in spring and again in fall.

Suggestions for Vigorous Growth
- Remove dead leaves from the center of plants—they'll quickly be replaced by new growth.

Easy Tip

To help bigroot geranium withstand drought, plant it in partial shade.

- Divide plants in early spring or fall, replanting divisions and watering well.
- Rosettes of new growth at points along the stems can be treated as cuttings and are easy to root—water them well after planting.

Pest Control
- No serious pests or diseases trouble this plant.

Complementary Plants
- Use as ground cover under summer-flowering shrubs such as butterfly bushes and roses.
- Combine with ferns, hostas, and small bulbs in a shady flower garden.

Recommended Selections
- 'Album' is a white-flowered selection.
- 'Biokovo', with white flowers flushed with pink at the center, does well here.

Blackberry Lily

Belamcanda chinensis

A Perennial with Pretty Flowers, Showy Seedpods, and Striking Foliage

In fall, blackberry lily forms shiny, round black seeds that look like clusters of blackberries inside their open pods. It sprouts everywhere, but it's as easy to control as it is to grow—just pull out the young plants you don't want. Blackberry lily is also called leopard flower for its orange flowers marked with red spots; they're star-shaped and last about two weeks. The irislike foliage provides a strong vertical accent in the flower garden.

Top Reasons to Plant

○ Showy flowers in summer
○ Ornamental seedpods in fall
○ Attractive foliage
○ Easy to grow
○ Self-seeds easily
○ Good cut flower
○ Adapts to variety of sites

Useful Hint

In dry soil and full sun, blackberry lily won't grow as tall—in rich, moist soil and light shade, it'll grow as tall as 4 feet and may need staking.

Bloom Color
Orange with red spots

Bloom Period
Summer

Height/Width
3 to 4 feet x 1 to 3 feet

Planting Location
• Prefers moist, well-drained soil with lots of organic matter, but tolerates average soil
• Sun or partial shade

Planting
• Set out plants in spring or early fall.
• Space plants 12 to 18 inches apart.
• Water well.
• Mulch heavily.

Watering
• For tallest growth, keep the soil constantly moist—plants are shorter in drier soils.

Fertilizing
• No fertilizer is needed.

Suggestions for Vigorous Growth
• No special care is required.

Easy Tip

For dried-flower decorations, harvest seedpods before they open completely.

Pest Control
• No serious pests or diseases trouble this plant.

Complementary Plants
• Grow with *Artemisia* 'Powis Castle'— which serves as a living trellis for the blackberry lily.
• Put in the middle or back of a perennial border next to other summer bloomers, such as daylilies, or next to foliage perennials, such as lamb's ears.

Recommended Selections
• *Belamcanda flabellata*, often sold as 'Hello Yellow', is shorter and has unspotted yellow flowers.

Black-Eyed Susan
Rudbeckia fulgida 'Goldsturm'

A Perennial Bright-Blooming Machine from Summer to Fall

A nationwide favorite that shows up in both formal landscapes and small cottage gardens, the black-eyed Susan called 'Goldsturm' blooms for weeks in summer. Quick to colonize by underground roots, it's easy to control in the garden. Unlike the annual black-eyed Susan that tolerates hot, dry soils, 'Goldsturm' prefers a moist, well-drained soil. Once established in the garden, it's a long-lived, easy-care perennial.

Top Reasons to Plant

○ Bright blossoms for many weeks
○ Insect and disease free
○ Easy to grow
○ Drought tolerant when established
○ Seedheads attract birds
○ Good cut flower
○ Low maintenance
○ Spreads quickly
○ Tolerates some shade

Useful Hint

Some *Rudbeckia* species, usually called coneflowers, may reach 5 to 7 feet tall and are very impressive—if you have room for them.

Bloom Color
Golden yellow

Bloom Period
Summer to fall

Height/Width
2 to 3 feet x 1 $^1/_2$ feet

Planting Location
• Well-drained, moderately fertile soil
• Full or partial sun

Planting
• Set out plants in spring or fall.
• Space 18 inches apart.
• Water well after planting.
• Mulch lightly.

Watering
• Water frequently to keep the root zone moist until the plants are established.
• Mature plants tolerate drought.

Fertilizing
• No fertilizer is needed except in very poor soil.

Suggestions for Vigorous Growth
• Remove spent flowers to prolong bloom.
• Divide black-eyed Susan every three years in spring or early fall.

Easy Tip
Dig up the offset and self-seeded plants, pot them, and give them away as gifts.

• Lift and replant offsets and new seedlings any time during the growing season.
• Keep well mulched.

Pest Control
• Spider mites may occur in very dry sites in midsummer; spray with water weekly to prevent them.
• Mildew may appear in late fall but is not a problem.

Complementary Plants
• Plant with ornamental grasses and sedum 'Autumn Joy'.

Recommended Selections
• *Rudbeckia nitida* 'Herbstonne' has large single yellow flowers with green rays—it grows to 7 feet tall and is wonderful in the fall garden.
• *Rudbeckia* 'Goldquelle' grows 2 to 3 feet tall with double yellow flowers in late summer.

Blanket Flower

Gaillardia × grandiflora

A Long-Blooming Perennial That Thrives in Heat

Blanket flower blooms from early summer until frost. In coastal areas of the state where soils are sandy, plants may bloom more profusely but won't grow as tall as they do in heavier soils. In clay soil, blanket flower is a short-lived perennial, but it reseeds itself freely, so don't worry if plants don't overwinter. Plants from seed won't be as uniform in size and color as named cultivars, but they'll produce some interesting color variations.

Top Reasons to Plant

○ Long season of bloom
○ Bright red and yellow flowers
○ Good cut flower
○ Drought resistant
○ Requires little care
○ Few insects and diseases bother it

Useful Hint

Unlike many perennials, blanket flowers grown from seed flower their first year—start seeds indoors six to eight weeks before the last expected frost.

Bloom Color
Red and yellow

Bloom Period
Summer to fall

Height/Width
2 to 3 feet x 1 to 2 feet

Planting Location
• Well-drained, moderately fertile soil
• Sun

Planting
• Set plants out in spring.
• Dig the hole as large as the plant's container.
• Set the plant at the same level it was growing previously.
• Firm the soil around the rootball.
• Water well.

Watering
• Keep the soil moist until plants are established—thereafter, they're drought tolerant.

Fertilizing
• No fertilizer is needed.

Suggestions for Vigorous Growth
• Remove spent flowers to promote longer blooming.
• Cut plants back in late summer to encourage a flush of growth and fall blooms.
• Transplant new growth that appears from the old crown.

Easy Tip

Blanket flower provides almost constant bloom in the flower border from early summer until fall.

Pest Control
• Root rot, crown rot, and mildew can be troublesome in poorly drained soils—be sure blanket flower has excellent drainage.

Complementary Plants
• Plant with sunflowers and other bold-textured and brightly colored flowers such as coreopsis, black-eyed Susan, and goldenrod.

Recommended Selections
• 'Goblin' is a popular dwarf cultivar with large dark-red flowers with wide, irregular yellow borders.
• 'Baby Cole' is another dwarf, growing only 6 to 8 inches tall.
• 'Red Plume' has double, bright-red flowers on a dense mound growing 12 to 14 inches tall.

Blazing Star

Liatris spicata

A Tough Native Perennial That Attracts Butterflies and Dazzles Gardeners

In summer, the colorful wands of blazing star, a native wildflower, attract butterflies and dazzle gardeners. A good choice for the flower border, meadow, or naturalistic garden, blazing star is also an outstanding cut flower, both fresh and dried. The vertical spikes are made of small flower heads that, unlike those of most flowers, open from the top down. Also called gayfeather, this native tolerates heat and drought, and is ideal for Georgia gardens.

Top Reasons to Plant

- Beautiful flowers
- Long bloom season
- Attracts butterflies
- Drought tolerant
- Thrives in heat
- Excellent cut or dried flower
- Provides vertical accent

Useful Hint

The bright flowers and linear foliage of blazing star provide a bold vertical accent in the garden.

Bloom Color
Purple or white

Bloom Period
Summer

Height/Width
36 inches x 6 to 12 inches

Planting Location
• Moderately fertile, moist, well-
  drained soil
• Sun or partial shade

Planting
• Set out plants in spring or fall.
• Dig the hole as large as the
  plant's container.
• Set the plant at the same level it
  was growing in the container.
• Firm the soil around the rootball.
• Water well.

Watering
• Provide an inch of water in weeks
  without that amount of rainfall.
• This plant tolerates wet soils during
  the growing season but not in winter.

Fertilizing
• No fertilizer is needed.

Easy Tip

Blazing star won't tolerate wet soil in
winter, so if you plant it along a
stream or pond, make sure it's an area
that dries out in winter.

Suggestions for Vigorous Growth
• Divide plants in spring every four years.
• After the first year, plants may
  need staking.

Pest Control
• No serious pests or diseases trouble
  this plant.

Complementary Plants
• Combine with black-eyed Susans
  and purple coneflower.

Recommended Selections
• 'Kobold', a compact cultivar 18 to
  30 inches tall, features dark-purple
  flowers—it's one of the best for cut
  flowers and the flower border.
• 'Floristan White' is 3 feet tall with
  creamy-white flowers.

Boltonia

Boltonia asteroides 'Snowbank'

A Cheerful White Perennial Daisy

Boltonia is an American native plant, and as a garden ornamental, the cultivar 'Snowbank' is much better behaved than the native species. Small, inch-wide white daisies with yellow centers cover the plant and look graceful against the gray-green linear foliage. Often the first blooms appear in August and continue well into September. Boltonia survives both periods of drought and soil conditions that are less than ideal.

Top Reasons to Plant

○ Masses of white daisies
○ Long season of bloom
○ Good cut flower
○ Attracts butterflies
○ Tolerates variety of conditions
○ Few insects or diseases
○ Drought tolerant

Useful Hint

To attract goldfinches to your yard, leave the plants standing after they've been killed by frost.

Bloom Color
White

Bloom Period
Late summer to fall

Height/Width
3 to 4 feet x 3 feet

Planting Location
• Prefers well-drained, moist, fertile soil but will tolerate poor to average soil
• Sun

Planting
• Set out plants in spring or fall.
• Dig the hole as large as the plant's container.
• Set the plant at the same level it was growing in the container.
• Firm the soil around the rootball.
• Water well.

Watering
• No watering is needed except in severe drought.

Fertilizing
• Feed the first spring.
• Beyond decaying mulch, no fertilizer is needed after the first year.

Easy Tip
To avoid having to stake boltonia, plant it in full sun.

Suggestions for Vigorous Growth
• Mulch with organic matter in spring and fall.
• Divide plants every two or three years when the clumps become large and begin to split open.

Pest Control
• No serious pests or diseases trouble this plant.

Complementary Plants
• Use in the middle or back of a flower border with aster, salvia, sedum, goldenrod, Joe-pye weed, and butterfly bush.
• Plant in naturalized areas with wildflowers such as swamp sunflower, ironweed, butterfly weed, bee balm, and black-eyed Susan.

Recommended Selections
• 'Pink Beauty' is a pink-flowered cultivar.

Butterfly Weed
Asclepias tuberosa

A Perennial Native Plant Beloved by Butterflies

Butterfly weed is a familiar wildflower along the same roadside ditches and open sunny fields that later display asters and goldenrod. Individual plants in one field may bloom in a whole range of colors, from yellow to orange to deep-red. A native, butterfly weed makes a good ornamental for the flower garden. And it's also a good meadow plant. The blooms are especially attractive to Aphrodite and Fritillary butterflies.

Top Reasons to Plant

○ Attracts butterflies
○ Beautiful, showy blooms
○ Easy care
○ Drought tolerant when established
○ Few pests and diseases
○ Good cut flower
○ Attractive dried seedpods for indoor use

Bloom Color
Orange, lipstick-red, or yellow

Bloom Period
Late spring to midsummer

Height/Width
1^1/$_2$ to 3 feet x 2 feet

Planting Location
- Average, well-drained soil—too much moisture, especially in winter, and the plant won't return the next spring
- Full sun—too little causes the plant to flop over
- Choose location with care; this plant's deep taproot usually breaks apart fatally when transplanting.

Planting
- Plant in early spring or fall.
- Space plants 10 to 12 inches apart.
- Transplant carefully to avoid breaking the taproot.
- Use a root-stimulating liquid fertilizer when planting.
- If growing from seeds, transplant when plants are very young and keep as much original soil attached as possible.

Watering
- This plant tolerates drought but does require water during long periods without rain.

Easy Tip

Don't dig butterfly weed from the wild—it's illegal, destructive, and the plant probably won't survive because its deep taproot is easily damaged.

Fertilizing
- No fertilizer is required.

Suggestions for Vigorous Growth
- Remove faded flowers to encourage a longer blooming time.
- Leave the second wave of flowers on the stems so the purple pods, which are great in flower arrangements, will open in late fall.
- Instead of dividing clumps, cut back plants to rejuvenate them.

Pest Control
- This plant is virtually free of pests and diseases.

Complementary Plants
- Use in a wildflower meadow.
- Locate toward the front of the border with shasta daisies, black-eyed Susans, and red hot pokers.

Recommended Selections
- Swamp milkweed (*Asclepias incarnata*) grows to 3 feet tall and has clusters of mauve, pink, or white flowers—it grows in dry or wet soils and attracts hordes of butterflies.

Useful Hint

Be sure you remember where you place this plant in the garden—it comes up late in the spring and might be mistaken for a weed or dug up before it sprouts.

Cardinal Flower

Lobelia cardinalis

A Gorgeous Late-Summer-Blooming Perennial Beloved by Hummingbirds

The list of cardinal flower's attributes makes it sound too good to be true. It grows in partial shade or shade, blooms in late summer when few other perennials do, produces tall spikes of brilliant red flowers much loved by hummingbirds, and self-sows so you always have a group of cardinal flowers. As if that weren't enough, it also stays in flower at least three weeks.

Top Reasons to Plant

- Hummingbirds love it
- Thrives in shade or partial shade
- Ideal for that always-damp spot in your yard
- Blooms in late summer when few other perennials do
- Has tall spikes of brilliant red flowers
- Self-seeds readily

Useful Hint

Plant cardinal flower in a shady corner near the house to bring hummingbirds into viewing range from a window.

Bloom Color
Red or pink

Bloom Period
Late summer

Height/Width
2 to 4 feet x 2 feet

Planting Location
- Rich, organic soil amended with compost or other material so it retains moisture
- Partial sun or shade

Planting
- Set plants out in spring.
- Space plants 18 to 24 inches apart.
- Mix pelleted, slow-release fertilizer into the planting hole.
- Water well after planting.
- Mulch well.

Watering
- Cardinal flower needs consistently moist soil, so watering enough is the key to success. Water when the top $1/2$ inch of soil is dry to the touch.
- Install a soaker hose to keep cardinal flower gently watered if it's in dry soil.

Fertilizing
- If a slow-release fertilizer was incorporated at planting, additional fertilizer usually isn't needed.
- If lower leaves turn yellow, spray with a water-soluble fertilizer made for flowering plants that contains iron.

Easy Tip

Cardinal flower is a great choice for a shady, soggy spot in your yard.

Suggestions for Vigorous Growth
- Pruning, pinching, and dividing are seldom needed.
- Pull back the mulch around this often short-lived plant after bloom to enable self-seeding.

Pest Control
- In the moist soil it loves, cardinal flower has few insects or diseases.
- If cardinal flower is growing in a dry area, aphids and spider mites may be a problem.
- Ask the Extension Service about controls, and water more often.

Complementary Plants
- Plant with flag iris near a water garden.

Recommended Selections
- 'Rose Beacon' has rosy-pink flowers on 40-inch stems.
- 'Shrimp Salad' is an unusual color for cardinal flowers—a soft, shrimp-pink.

Coleus

Solenostemon scutellarioides

A Newly Trendy Old-Fashioned Annual with Gorgeous Foliage

It used to be that coleus came in dark-red and a few other colors, and you used it when you couldn't think of anything else to grow in the shade. With the myriad hybrids available today, coleus is no longer a last resort when it comes to choosing annuals with beautiful foliage for shade and sun. Available in every color and color combination, plants range in size from dwarf and bushy to tall and tropical-looking.

Top Reasons to Plant

○ Beautiful foliage in brilliant color combinations
○ Excellent in containers or in the garden
○ Varieties for sun and shade
○ Usually pest and disease free
○ Combines well with other annuals and with perennials
○ Easy to grow
○ Roots readily from cuttings to produce more plants

Useful Hint

While most coleus are happiest in partial shade where their colors are more vivid, some varieties thrive in summer sun.

Bloom Color
Foliage in shades of red, pink, gold, chartreuse, and bicolors

Bloom Period
Foliage effective from spring until frost

Height/Width
6 to 48 inches x 8 to 36 inches

Planting Location
• Moist, well-drained soil amended with organic matter to improve drainage
• Some tolerate more sun than others, so check the plant label to see whether it's a sun or shade coleus
• In containers, make sure the soil mix is light but has enough organic matter to hold moisture

Planting
• Set out plants after all chance of spring frost has passed.
• Space plants 6 to 18 inches apart, depending on mature size.
• Mix pelleted, slow-release fertilizer with the soil in the planting hole.
• Water well.
• Mulch with 1 to 1¹/₂ inches of organic matter.

Watering
• Water regularly so coleus plants do not dry out.
• Be especially careful to water plants daily in containers and hanging baskets.

Fertilizing
• If you are growing coleus in containers, add Osmocote® to the planting mix and apply a liquid fertilizer once a month.

Easy Tip
Coleus can be easily rooted from stem cuttings and overwintered indoors—they can also be started from seeds indoors in early spring.

Suggestions for Vigorous Growth
• Pinch plants and flower buds back regularly, once a month or more, to keep coleus full and bushy.

Pest Control
• Watch for snails and slugs; if they appear, ask at a garden center about organic controls for them.

Complementary Plants
• Plant in shade gardens to add easy-care seasonal color to evergreen ferns.

Recommended Selections
• Fairway series, extra-compact dwarf plants for shade, comes in many colors.
• The Wizard series offers large, heart-shaped leaves; with plants growing 12 to 14 inches, they are suited for hanging baskets, containers, and shady landscapes.

Columbine
Aquilegia canadensis

A Graceful, Colorful Perennial That Shouts "Spring Is Here!"

Though this columbine's flowers are not as showy as those of some hybrids, this vigorous native seeds itself freely and delights us when it appears in the most unlikely places— between rocks, in tiny crevices, or in the cavities of dead trees. The 1-inch delicate flowers bloom on and off for several weeks. *Aquilegia canadensis* seems more resistant to leaf miners than are many of the large-flowered selections.

Top Reasons to Plant

○ Beautiful two-toned flowers
○ Flowers with unusual shape
○ Attracts butterflies and hummingbirds
○ Mixes well with both spring wildflowers and border plants
○ Grows nicely in partial shade
○ Reseeds readily

Useful Hint

Plant columbines at the front of a border or along a path where their delicate nature can be appreciated.

40

Bloom Color
Red and yellow, bell-shaped, nodding

Bloom Period
Early spring

Height/Width
2 to 3 feet x 1 foot

Planting Location
- Rich organic soil that holds moisture but drains rapidly
- Partial shade or sun with plenty of moisture

Planting
- Set out early spring or fall.
- Space plants about 1 foot apart.
- Water well after planting.
- Mulch to cool soil and hold moisture, but do not bury the crown of the plant.

Watering
- Water when soil is dry to the touch..

Fertilizing
- Columbine doesn't usually need fertilizer—the mulch breaks down, gently feeding the plant.

Suggestions for Vigorous Growth
- Columbine rarely lives more than a few years but reseeds itself.
- To avoid reseeding, remove flowers as they fade.
- *Or* deadhead the first flowers to encourage more blooms, then allow the second blooms to set seed.
- If mature clumps need dividing, do it after bloom, carefully teasing apart

Easy Tip

Let the last wave of flowers set seeds; then pull back the mulch around the plants so you'll have a new supply of plants next spring.

sections of the main plant, making sure each division has buds and some roots.

Pest Control
- Columbine is subject to attack by leaf miners, which leave little "trails" on the foliage—an easy control is to cut back the foliage as soon as you see damage; the plants then put out a new flush of leaves that look good until frost.

Complementary Plants
- Combine columbines with perennials that flower later in the year, such as asters in sun or ferns and hostas in shade.
- Use with Siberian iris and other spring bloomers.

Recommended Selections
- *Aquilegia canadensis* 'Corbett', a yellow-flowered cultivar, is 12 to 24 inches tall.
- *Aquilegia flabellata* var. *nana* is a good dwarf, growing fewer than 12 inches tall, and is excellent for the front of a border or a rock garden.

Cosmos

Cosmos bipinnatus, Cosmos sulphureus

Cheerful Annuals Anyone Can Grow

For drought-resistant beauty, *Cosmos sulphureus*, yellow cosmos, is hard to beat. This adaptable annual blooms for weeks and, once established, requires very little moisture. The bold flowers of yellow, gold, golden-orange, or scarlet-orange seem to dance in the breeze. The largest flowered cosmos is *Cosmos bipinnatus*, whose blooms measure 4 to 6 inches across and come in shades of pink, red, white, and crimson.

Top Reasons to Plant

○ Easy, easy, easy
○ Heavy bloomer
○ Good cut flower
○ Reseeds readily
○ Essential for both cottage gardens and natural landscapes
○ Drought resistant when established
○ Few pests and diseases

Useful Hint

Cosmos is so easy to grow that many highway departments use them along roadways.

Bloom Color
Yellow, orange, red, pink, or white

Bloom Period
Summer to frost

Height/Width
2 to 6 feet x 1 to 2^1/$_2$ feet

Planting Location
- Well-drained, poor to average soil
- Full sun
- Protection from wind for taller types

Planting
- Start seeds indoors two to three weeks before the last expected frost.
- Sow seeds in single pots rather than flats to avoid disturbing the roots.
- *Or* sow seeds outdoors in a sunny spot after all danger of frost has passed and the soil is warm.
- Space homegrown or nursery plants 12 to 18 inches apart.
- Water with a root stimulator after planting.
- Mulch lightly or not at all to encourage reseeding.

Watering
- Water regularly until plants are about 8 inches high.
- Mature plants need little watering, but soak the soil well each time you do water.

Fertilizing
- Feed young seedlings with liquid 10-10-10 fertilizer at three-fourths the recommended rate.
- Avoid overfertilizing—too much fertilizer or over-rich soil causes weak stems.

Easy Tip

Avoid windy sites for tall cosmos, or you'll have to stake them.

Suggestions for Vigorous Growth
- For maximum flowers, pinch back tall varieties when they reach 12 to 18 inches tall.
- Snip off faded blooms to keep the flowers coming.

Pest Control
- If aphids are a problem, spray them with insecticidal soap or a blast of water.

Complementary Plants
- Plant with gray and silver foliage plants, such as lamb's ear or artemisia.
- Combine with spiky flowers, such as liatris.

Recommended Selections
- *Cosmos bipinnatus* 'Sea Shells' has fluted petals in creamy white, pink, and crimson.
- 'Early Sensation' is a tall selection growing from 3 to 4 feet with flowers of crimson, rose, pink, or white.
- *Cosmos sulphureus* Ladybird series is a dwarf group growing to 12 inches tall with flowers in orange, scarlet, and a mixture.

Crocosmia
Crocosmia hybrids

A Summer Afternoon Delight

This native of tropical and southern Africa has bold foliage that provides a striking vertical accent in the garden. Arching spikes of bright, cheerful flowers appear to delight us in summer with red, orange, or yellow blooms that are 1 to 1½ inches in diameter. These sturdy plants add excitement to the garden and make exotic cut flowers. The old-fashioned species *Crocosmia crocosmiiflora*, known as montbretia, still exists in old gardens where it has seeded itself.

Top Reasons to Plant

○ Beautiful flowers
○ Exotic appearance
○ Attracts hummingbirds
○ Thrives in heat
○ Excellent cut flower
○ Provides vertical accent

Useful Hint

Trim the foliage back if it looks bad at the end of the summer, and cut it back to the ground in autumn.

Bloom Color
Red, orange, or yellow

Bloom Period
Summer

Height/Width
2 to 4 feet x 2 to 3 feet

Planting Location
• Fertile, moist, well-drained soil
• Sun or partial shade

Planting
• Set out plants in spring or fall.
• Dig the hole as large as the plant's container.
• Set the plant at the same level it was growing previously.
• Firm the soil around the rootball.
• Water well.
• Mulch with 1/2 inch of organic matter.

Watering
• Water weekly during the first growing season.
• In subsequent years, water every two weeks.

Fertilizing
• Feed after planting in spring with 10-10-10.
• Topdress with organic matter once every spring and fall.

Easy Tip

If you plant crocosmia on a slope, you'll be better able to appreciate the dangling blooms.

Suggestions for Vigorous Growth
• If the soil is too rich, plants will put out lots of floppy foliage.
• If clumps are large and the flowers flop over, divide clumps in early spring.
• Replant and water immediately after dividing the clumps.

Pest Control
• Spider mites may appear and can be controlled with insecticidal soap.

Complementary Plants
• Combine with black-eyed Susans, daylilies, and deep blue veronica.

Recommended Selections
• 'Lucifer' is a striking hybrid that grows 4 feet tall with bright red flowers.

Fan Flower

Scaevola 'Blue Wonder'

A Lovely Annual Perfect for Containers and Ground Cover

When it blooms, fan flower looks like a profusion of tiny purple-blue fans marked with yellow. Some gardeners think the flowers look more purple, but others describe them as blue. For long-season bloom and easy care, this Australian transplant gets our vote as one of the top ten annuals for Georgia gardens. It may even be perennial in the most southern parts of the state. The hotter it gets, the more it seems to thrive.

Top Reasons to Plant

○ Long blooming season
○ Tolerates heat and humidity
○ Excellent in hanging baskets
○ Few pests and diseases
○ Excellent range of colors
○ Attracts butterflies
○ Combines well in containers with other annuals

Useful Hint

When you head to the garden center for plants, ask for skuh-VOH-luh, which is also called fan flower for the shape of its blooms.

Bloom Color
Blue to purple to violet

Bloom Period
Summer until frost

Height/Width
6 to 12 inches x 12 to 24 inches

Planting Location
- Well-drained soil enriched with organic matter
- Sun or light shade

Planting
- Set out in spring after the soil has warmed up.
- Place two or three plants into a hanging basket.
- Mix pelleted, slow-release fertilizer into the soil at planting time.
- Water well.
- Use pine straw to mulch beds.

Watering
- Keep the soil moist—the plant stops growing and blooming unless well watered.
- Do not let the soil in the garden or containers dry out.

Fertilizing
- Feed garden plants monthly and container plants twice a month with a water-soluble plant food made for flowers.

Easy Tip
Place pots of scaevola on top of a wall, and let them cascade over.

Suggestions for Vigorous Growth
- Pinch tips lightly to promote bushiness when plants have 3 inches of new growth.
- Continue pinching occasionally through midsummer.
- If plants get too leggy, cut them back.
- Keep plants mulched in flower beds.
- To bring this plant indoors for the winter, cut it back to encourage new growth and then pot the cuttings.

Pest Control
- Few pests bother scaevola.

Complementary Plants
- Pair scaevola with gray, yellow, pink, and other blue flowered plants.

Recommended Selections
- 'Blue Fans' has sky-blue flowers with white eyes.
- 'Blue Shamrock' is the most intense blue so far.

Fragrant Hosta

Hosta × 'Royal Standard'

A Sun-Loving Perennial with Showy Leaves and Fragrant Blooms

While many hostas resist heat, few tolerate full sun. But 'Royal Standard', an adaptable hybrid of the old-fashioned favorite *Hosta plantaginea*, grows happily in full sun or shade, forming large mounds up to 3 feet wide of bold, yellow-green, deeply veined foliage. Worth growing for the foliage alone, this hosta also rewards us with sweetly scented flowers in late summer.

Top Reasons to Plant

- Handsome large leaves
- Fragrant white blossoms
- Thrives in sun or partial shade
- Few pests or diseases
- Excellent cut flower and foliage
- Attracts butterflies
- Good interplanted with daffodils to hide dying foliage

Useful Hint

Although 'Royal Standard' will survive in compacted or dry soils, the plants will be stunted and the leaves discolored.

Bloom Color
White

Bloom Period
Late summer

Height/Width
2 to 3 feet x 2 to 3 feet

Planting Location
• Rich, moist, well-drained soil
• Sun to partial shade

Planting
• Set plants out in early spring or fall.
• Space hostas 2 to 3 feet apart to accommodate their mature spread.
• Fertilize with a pelleted, slow-release fertilizer worked into each planting hole.
• Water well after planting.
• Mulch well unless slugs are known to be a problem.

Watering
• Water deeply during periods of drought.

Fertilizing
• No fertilizer is needed if the soil has lots of rich, organic matter.

Suggestions for Vigorous Growth
• Remove flower stalks as soon as hostas finish blooming and before they set seed.
• If foliage becomes unsightly early in the season, shear plants back to encourage new growth.
• Early spring is best for dividing hostas, but it can be done anytime of year if the plants are watered well and quickly replanted.

Easy Tip

Plant 'Royal Standard' near pathways where you can appreciate the fragrant flowers in late summer.

Pest Control
• Slugs may attack hostas, turning their leaves into an ugly mass of holes—try mulching with pine straw, or contact your Extension Agent about recommended controls.

Complementary Plants
• Use as a ground cover or interplant with spring bulbs, such as daffodils— the unfurling hosta leaves hide the dying foliage of the bulbs.

Recommended Selections
• Hostas range from a few inches tall— such as *Hosta venusta*, with its 1- to 2-inch leaves—to those like 'Sum and Substance', with mature plants up to 6 feet wide—the latter is chartreuse and tolerates sun, adding interesting texture and color to the garden.

Geranium

Pelargonium species and hybrids

A Favorite Showy Annual Great for Containers

It's hard to imagine a summer without geraniums. Many gardeners grow them in containers so they can be moved to the porch during long rainy spells, when they would otherwise stop blooming and sulk. But now seed-grown varieties in interesting colors are available, inexpensive, and small enough for you to plant a bed of just geraniums. These usually are sold in packs of four or six.

Top Reasons to Plant

- Bright, showy clusters of blooms
- Wide range of colors
- Long blooming season
- Good in window boxes and planters
- Attracts hummingbirds
- Roots easily for indoor potted plants in winter

Useful Hint

In the cooler parts of the state, try delicate-looking ivy geraniums in hanging baskets.

Bloom Color
Red, orange, salmon, pink, lavender, or white; some mottled or bicolored

Bloom Period
Spring until fall

Height/Width
12 to 36 inches x 14 to 24 inches

Planting Location
• Rich, moist soil amended with organic matter to ensure good drainage for garden plantings
• Morning sun and afternoon shade
• Ivy geraniums need mostly shade, especially in hotter areas of the state.

Planting
• For containers, use a packaged potting mix.
• Space plants so air circulates between them—1 to 2 feet apart depending on the type.
• Work a pelleted, slow-release fertilizer into the soil.
• Water well after planting.
• Mulch lightly.

Watering
• Water regularly so soil never dries out.

Fertilizing
• Feed geraniums in pots weekly with a water-soluble fertilizer made for blooming plants.
• Place more pelleted, slow-release fertilizer around bedding geraniums in midsummer.

Easy Tip
Take cuttings in fall—they root easily—and overwinter in a sunny windowsill or greenhouse for first flowers next spring.

Suggestions for Vigorous Growth
• The key to success is pinching the tips of young plants regularly to make them branch and thus produce more flowers.
• If stems rot in garden plantings, dig up the plants, dispose of them, and don't plant another geranium in the same spot.
• Keep old flowers cut off to encourage new blooms.

Pest Control
• If leaves turn yellow, spray with chelated iron.

Complementary Plants
• Mix with dusty miller in containers, letting *Vinca major* trail over the edges.

Recommended Selections
• 'Eyes Right' has pink blooms accented with a red eye.

Globe Amaranth

Gomphrena globosa

An Annual That Laughs at Georgia Heat and Humidity

An old-fashioned favorite, globe amaranth blooms all summer in Georgia gardens. In the autumn, when many annuals look tired and worn out, it blooms and blooms some more, until finally the plants are killed by a hard frost. The flowers hold their magenta color well, not only in the garden, but also in flower arrangements both fresh and dried. All this dependable annual requires is lots of sun and a well-drained soil.

Top Reasons to Plant

○ Tolerates heat and humidity
○ Bushels of blooms all summer long
○ Good cut flower
○ Good dried flower
○ Easy to grow
○ Drought tolerant when established

Useful Hint

For flower arrangers, the Woodcreek series offers colors in shades of purple, silver, white, and pink, with plants 24 to 30 inches tall.

Bloom Color
White, purple, pink, or red

Bloom Period
Summer to frost

Height/Width
10 to 24 inches x 12 to 16 inches

Planting Location
• Moist, well-drained soil with organic matter and coarse sand added to improve drainage in heavy soils
• Full sun

Planting
• Plant after the weather is consistently warm—usually May.
• Space plants 1 foot apart.
• Mix pelleted, slow-release fertilizer into the soil in the planting hole.
• Water well after planting.
• Mulch lightly.

Watering
• Once established, plants need water only during dry spells.

Fertilizing
• Fertilize seldom, and if slow-release fertilizer was used at planting, not at all.

Suggestions for Vigorous Growth
• Cut flowers for drying just when they've fully opened, and hang them upside down in a warm, dry place.

Easy Tip

The blooms dry right on the plant and can be used for winter arrangements.

Pest Control
• Stippled leaves may mean spider mites.
• Test for spider mites by holding a piece of white paper under the suspected leaf and thumping the leaf. If the "dust" that falls begins to move, it's spider mites.
• Pick off affected leaves, and remove severely infested plants.
• Prevent spider mites by spraying water on the foliage once a week.

Complementary Plants
• Plant with other heat-lovers such as lantana and verbena 'Homestead Purple'.
• Combine the dark-fuchsia types with purple foliage plants such as *Alternanthera* 'Wave Hill'.

Recommended Selections
• The Buddy series offers 9-inch-tall plants for bedding, edging, or cut flowers in reddish purple or white.
• *Gomphrena haageana* 'Strawberry Fields' has bright-red flowers and grows 2 feet tall.

Hardy Begonia
Begonia grandis (evansiana)

A Carefree Perennial for Light or Deep Shade

The elegant hardy begonia is like Cinderella waiting to be discovered, while the gaudy stepsisters, wax begonias, get all the attention. A true patrician, hardy begonia waits until late in the season to put on a show. The waxy leaves look fresh all season, especially when late afternoon light hits the red undersides from behind. Airy sprays of pink flowers rise above the foliage in August and bloom for weeks.

Top Reasons to Plant

○ Dainty sprays of flowers
○ Long season of bloom
○ Elegant foliage
○ Ornamental seed capsules
○ Thrives in shade
○ Adaptable to different soils
○ Few pests and diseases
○ Reseeds itself

Useful Hint

After bloom is over, leave the blossoms to develop into ornamental dried-seed capsules that last into the winter.

Bloom Color
Pink

Bloom Period
Late summer to fall

Height/Width
18 to 24 inches x 24 inches

Planting Location
• Cool, moist, well-drained, moderately fertile soil
• Partial shade or shade

Planting
• Set out plants in spring.
• Space plants 18 to 24 inches apart.
• Water well.
• Mulch well.

Watering
• Provide an inch of water each week if there hasn't been that amount of rainfall.

Fertilizing
• When new growth emerges in spring, feed with a pelleted, slow-release fertilizer.

Suggestions for Vigorous Growth
• If plants become leggy, cut them back in late spring so they'll be bushy by fall when they begin blooming.

Easy Tip

It's a good idea to draw a map of where you plant hardy begonia since it comes up very late in the spring.

• Little bulbils in the leaf axils will reseed—or you may remove them and set them in potting soil to root and create new plants.
• Keep well mulched year-round.

Pest Control
• No serious pests or diseases trouble this plant.

Complementary Plants
• Use as a ground cover under spring-blooming shrubs or plant with other shade-loving perennials.
• For an excellent effect, combine with evergreen ferns, such as the autumn fern and Christmas fern.

Recommended Selections
• *Begonia grandis* 'Alba' has white flowers.

Hardy Lantana

Lantana camara 'Miss Huff'

A Long-Blooming Southern Favorite That Attracts Hordes of Butterflies

Lantana has long been a favorite of Southern gardeners, not only because it's easy to grow, but because it blooms all summer and attracts hordes of butterflies. Fairly drought-resistant, 'Miss Huff' is said to be hardier than many other lantanas. Clusters of yellow, orange, and red flowers cover plants for months in hot, humid weather.

Top Reasons to Plant

- Showy bright flowers
- Long season of bloom
- Needs little care
- Tolerates dry soils
- Few pests and diseases
- Thrives in heat and sun
- Does well in containers

Useful Hint

Few perennials require so little care and bloom over such a long period as 'Miss Huff.'

Bloom Color
Yellow, orange, and red

Bloom Period
Summer to frost

Height/Width
3 to 6 feet x 3 to 5 feet

Planting Location
• Well-drained, average garden soil
• Sun
• Containers

Planting
• Set out plants in spring.
• Space plants 2 to 3 feet apart.
• Water well.

Watering
• In containers, water regularly.
• In the garden, water during extended drought periods once the plant is well established.

Fertilizing
• In the garden, feed with liquid 10-10-10 fertilizer after planting.
• In containers, fertilize monthly during the growing season.

Suggestions for Vigorous Growth
• Cut plants back as needed during the summer.
• At the end of the growing season, don't cut back the plants—instead mulch well with pine straw and cut them back in early spring just before new growth begins.
• Avoid planting in areas that stay wet in winter.

Easy Tip

Lantana branches sometimes root in place, providing additional instant plants to share with others.

Pest Control
• No serious pests or diseases trouble this plant.

Complementary Plants
• Plant in a big mass on a sunny slope.
• Mix with other summer-flowering annuals and perennials.

Recommended Selections
• Annual types of lantanas come in many colors and forms—'Irene' has rose-and-yellow flowers, 'New Gold' has golden-yellow flowers, 'Lemon Drop' has light-yellow flowers, and there are trailing varieties with lavender or white flowers.

Impatiens

Impatiens walleriana

An Annual That Provides Super Color in the Shade

Impatiens is one of the few annuals that you may actually be ready to pull out before it stops blooming. If the flowers are happy where they grow, next year you'll probably be treated to volunteer seedlings that plant themselves everywhere. Once they're 2 or 3 inches high, impatiens plants are easy to transplant or pull out. Impatiens grows under trees where it's often difficult to get anything to live, let alone bloom all summer.

Top Reasons to Plant

- Lots of flowers in lots of colors
- Loves shade
- Easy to grow
- Few pests and diseases
- Long season of bloom
- Doesn't require deadheading—it's self-cleaning!
- Cuttings root easily to produce more plants
- Attracts hummingbirds and butterflies

Bloom Color
White, pink, rose, lavender, red, orange, salmon, or bicolors

Bloom Period
Summer to frost

Height/Width
6 to 18 inches x 8 to 24 inches

Planting Location
• Rich, well-drained, moist soil enriched with organic matter
• Shade or partial shade
• Containers

Planting
• Set plants out after all chance of frost has passed.
• Place plants about 10 inches apart.
• Mix pelleted, slow-release fertilizer into the soil.
• Water well after planting.
• Mulch with 2 inches of organic mulch.

Watering
• Keep the soil constantly moist.
• Consider watering impatiens with a soaker hose if they are under trees.

Fertilizing
• Every month during the growing season, apply a water-soluble fertilizer made for blooming plants.

Easy Tip
Some of the best varieties of impatiens have been passed down from one generation to the next.

Suggestions for Vigorous Growth
• Ample water and fertilization are the keys to success.
• Pinch plants back any time they look leggy.

Pest Control
• Slugs may appear in wet weather.
• Spider mites may appear in very dry weather.
• Ask your garden center or Extension Agent about chemical controls if homemade traps don't control the slugs and spraying the plants with water doesn't get rid of the spider mites.

Complementary Plants
• Use impatiens with ferns and hostas on the sunny edge of a woodland.

Recommended Selections
• Super Elfin series grows 8 to 10 inches tall and comes in fifteen different colors.
• The Sun and Shade series offers strong growers for pots, baskets, window boxes, and bedding plants—it comes in seventeen different colors.
• Impatiens 'Rose Parade' has semidouble flowers, in brilliant colors, on plants growing 2 feet tall.

Useful Hint
Impatiens makes beautiful hanging baskets, especially if you keep plants full by pinching them back.

Japanese Anemone

Anemone × hybrida 'Honorine Jobert'

A Fall-Blooming Perennial of Delicate Beauty

An elegant fall bloomer, the white Japanese anemone brightens up the garden at the end of the day. Popular since before the Civil War, 'Honorine Jobert' is still a favorite selection of gardeners who don't live in coastal areas. A strong grower, it produces a large mound of foliage in summer, topped in fall by slender, stately 3-foot stems with beautiful white 2- to 3-inch flowers that dance in the autumn breezes.

Top Reasons to Plant

○ Beautiful, fresh blooms in fall
○ Does well in partial shade
○ Insect and disease free
○ Spreads quickly in a spot it likes
○ Requires little maintenance
○ Brightens shade plantings of hostas and ferns
○ Flowers sway on long stems in the slightest breeze
○ Good cut flower

Useful Hint

Experiment to find the ideal soil for anemones—they need excellent winter drainage but consistent moisture during the growing season.

Bloom Color
White

Bloom Period
Early fall

Height/Width
3 to 4 feet x 2 to 3 feet

Planting Location
- Rich, well-drained soil in a naturally moist spot—or water often
- Best in partial shade, preferably morning sun

Planting
- Plant in early spring or early fall.
- Amend soil with organic matter to add fertility and improve drainage.
- Space plants 1 to 2 feet apart.
- Water thoroughly after planting.
- Mulch well, and keep mulch at a 2-inch thickness.

Watering
- Keep soil evenly moist at all times.
- Anemone cannot tolerate drought.
- A site that includes standing water over the winter will kill anemone.

Fertilizing
- Topdress with organic matter in spring and fall.

Easy Tip

In the garden, white can either soften intense hues or help show them off.

Suggestions for Vigorous Growth
- Provide anemone the moisture it requires.
- Keep it mulched well to preserve moisture.
- Divide clumps every three years.
- Stake tall stems to avoid damage from thunderstorms.

Pest Control
- Anemone has few pest or disease problems.

Complementary Plants
- Combine with gray foliage plants, such as artemisia or lamb's ears.
- For contrast, plant with rich-purple asters.

Recommended Selections
- 'Whirlwind' has semidouble white flowers.
- *Anemone hupehensis* 'September Charm' has pink flowers and grows 2 to 3 feet high—it isn't nearly as elegant as the white forms but is still worth growing.

Japanese Roof Iris
Iris tectorum

A Striking, Vigorous, Adaptable Perennial

Georgia gardeners may be pleasantly surprised to learn that the ideal climate for growing Japanese roof iris is one of hot summers and moderately cold winters. While these flowers, which were grown on thatched roofs in Japan, don't grow on roofs in our climate, Japanese roof iris is a vigorous, adaptable perennial that grows happily all over the state. Its pale-green foliage grows fanlike, and the lilac flowers have white crests in place of beards.

Top Reasons to Plant

- Pretty blooms
- Striking foliage
- Easy to grow
- Tolerates heat and humidity
- Few pests and diseases
- Spreads rapidly in light, sandy soils

Useful Hint

Japanese roof iris is especially fond of the light, sandy soils in our coastal areas, where it grows like a weed.

Bloom Color
Lilac or white

Bloom Period
Summer

Height/Width
12 to 18 inches x 12 to 18 inches

Planting Location
- Prefers moderately fertile, light, well-drained soil
- Sun or partial shade

Planting
- Plant anytime during the growing season.
- Set plants 12 to 18 inches apart.
- Lightly cover the plant's rhizomes.
- Water well.
- Mulch.

Watering
- Well-established plants should need water only during drought periods.

Fertilizing
- No fertilizer is needed if the soil is moderately fertile and plants are top-dressed with organic mulch in spring and fall.

Easy Tip
Japanese roof iris may not produce as many blooms in a shady garden, but its light-green, fanlike foliage adds a touch of elegance.

Suggestions for Vigorous Growth
- Keep mulch away from the plant's crown.
- Cut tattered foliage back to a few inches in early spring, and new leaves will quickly replace the old.

Pest Control
- No serious pests or diseases trouble this plant.

Complementary Plants
- Plant near the front of the flower border with other summer-bloomers.

Recommended Selections
- *Iris tectorum* 'Alba' has white flowers and is equally elegant.
- *Iris cristata*, which is like a miniature form of Japanese roof iris, does well in our climate—it grows in woodlands and adapts well to the shade garden.

Joe-Pye Weed

Eupatorium purpureum

A Bold, Architectural Perennial Statement

A classic American native, Joe-pye weed grows along roadsides, in meadows, and in fields from Maine to Georgia. A perfect choice for a bold, architectural statement in the perennial border, Joe-pye can grow 5 to 7 feet tall, so give it room. The large purple flower heads, up to 18 inches in diameter, are showy for weeks beginning in early fall. The 8- to 12-inch-long whorled leaves are impressive even when the plant isn't in bloom.

Top Reasons to Plant

- Huge, showy flowers
- Large dramatic scale
- Easy to grow
- Few pests and diseases
- Attracts butterflies and hummingbirds
- Loves moisture

Useful Hint

Joe-pye weed is a good focal point in the fall garden, attracting butterflies and eliciting admiring comments as its big masses of flowers sway in the breeze.

64

Bloom Color
Pinkish purple

Bloom Period
Fall

Height/Width
5 to 7 feet x 3 to 4 feet

Planting Location
- Prefers moist soil but adapts to a wide variety of conditions
- Sun to light shade

Planting
- Plant in spring or early fall.
- Set plants 2 to 3 feet apart.
- Water well.
- Mulch well.

Watering
- Provide an inch of water per week if there hasn't been that much rainfall and if the plant isn't in a naturally moist spot.

Fertilizing
- No fertilizer is needed.

Suggestions for Vigorous Growth
- Divide clumps every two or three years.
- For a more compact plant, cut back plants in early summer.
- Cut plants to the ground after blooming ends.

Easy Tip

If you have a small garden, look at the newer, shorter cultivars of Joe-pye weed such as 'Galaxy' and 'Gateway'.

Pest Control
- No serious pests or diseases trouble this plant.

Complementary Plants
- Plant with cardinal flower, swamp sunflower, ironweed, and Tartarian aster.
- Use as an accent plant at the back of a large flower border.
- Incorporate into naturalized plantings, such as meadows or along streams.

Recommended Selections
- *Eupatorium maculatum* 'Gateway' is a smaller cultivar that grows 5 to 6 feet tall—it has large, mauve-pink flowers atop reddish stems.

Lenten Rose

Helleborus orientalis

A Shade-Loving Perennial That Blooms in Winter

Aristocrats of the garden, hellebores bridge the gap from winter to spring. These elegant evergreens have shiny, leathery 12- to 16-inch-wide leaves divided into seven to nine segments. One of the gems of the winter garden, lenten rose looks good all year. Its colorful, nodding flowers, ranging from pure-white to dark-maroon and sometimes speckled or splotched with green or purple, appear as early as February; the plant may produce flowers for eight to ten weeks.

Top Reasons to Plant

○ Late-winter blooms
○ Loves shade
○ Pest and disease free
○ Reseeds freely
○ Good cut flower
○ Easy to grow
○ Flowers change color as they mature
○ Handsome foliage after bloom

Useful Hint

Helleborus leaves and roots are poisonous, which may explain why animals leave it alone in the garden.

Bloom Color
White, purple, or maroon

Bloom Period
Late winter to spring

Height/Width
14 to 18 inches x 12 to 18 inches

Planting Location
- Well-drained, deep, fertile soil amended with organic matter
- Full to partial shade
- Avoid winter sun, which burns the leaves and flowers

Planting
- Set out container-grown plants in early spring or early fall.
- Transplant seedlings from around established mature plants when they're 4 inches tall—keep as much dirt as possible around the roots.
- Space plants 18 to 24 inches apart.
- Mulch with organic matter, such as pine straw.

Watering
- Plant in moisture-retaining soil that's mulched; lenten roses prefer consistent moisture but are surprisingly tolerant of dry weather.
- Water enough to keep the soil moist when the plants are young and during droughts.

Fertilizing
- Using 10-10-10, fertilize after planting the first spring.

Easy Tip
Once you plant lenten rose, you'll have it forever because it reseeds, though not aggressively—even producing new color combinations.

Suggestions for Vigorous Growth
- Evergreen leaves can sometimes suffer winter damage; clip them off as flowers appear so the flowers can shine.
- Lenten rose grows slowly and seldom needs dividing.
- Pull mulch back as seeds mature to allow the plants to reseed.

Pest Control
- Lenten rose has no serious pests.

Complementary Plants
- Plant with ferns and hostas in the shade garden.
- Use as a ground cover with daffodils—it shows off their spring flowers and masks their ugly summer foliage.

Recommended Selections
- *Helleborus foetidus* has pale-green flowers edged in maroon.
- *Helleborus argutifolius* has a coarse, hollylike texture and chartreuse flowers streaked with purple.

Mexican Sunflower

Tithonia rotundifolia

A Majestic Heat-Loving Annual with Intense Orange Daisies

We remember driving by an old country garden in south Georgia and marveling at some small flowering trees with intense orange daisies that were thriving despite the red clay soil. The plants appeared larger than the house whose door they framed—they looked like living torches. They may have been only 7 feet tall, but the effect was dramatic. Mexican sunflower has a coarse texture and vibrant orange flowers that attract butterflies to the summer garden.

Top Reasons to Plant

- Bright-orange flowers
- Attracts butterflies and hummingbirds
- Good cut flower
- Thrives in heat and humidity
- Tall and dramatic
- Few pests and diseases

Useful Hint

Mexican sunflower makes a good screen or summer hedge; when placed in groups, the plants support each other—minimizing the need for staking.

Bloom Color
Orange-scarlet

Bloom Period
Summer

Height/Width
4 to 7 feet x 3 to 4 feet

Planting Location
- Prefers moderately fertile soil but adapts to almost any soil
- Sun

Planting
- Sow seeds in the garden after all danger of frost has passed—the strongest plants are those grown directly from seeds.
- Keep the seedbed moist until plants are up and growing well.
- Thin plants to stand between 2 and 4 feet apart.

Watering
- Water deeply during periods of drought.

Fertilizing
- Feed lightly with a liquid fertilizer once or twice during the growing season.

Suggestions for Vigorous Growth
- Plants may need staking if they're not rooted well or watered thoroughly.

Easy Tip

Site Mexican sunflower at the middle or back of the border where its large scale can be appreciated.

Pest Control
- No serious pests or diseases trouble this plant.

Complementary Plants
- Plant as a companion for black-eyed Susan, Joe-pye weed, and dark-purple selections of the butterfly bush.
- Mix in with other sunflowers.

Recommended Selections
- There are a number of dwarf cultivars, including 'Goldfinger', which grows 2 to 3 feet tall; 'Torch', which grows to 3 to 4 feet; and 'Yellow Torch', which grows 3 to 4 feet tall and has yellow flowers.

Moss Phlox

Phlox subulata

A Bright, Bold Perennial for an Early-Spring Show

Moss phlox is just the plant for gardeners who want bright, bold colors. Forget those subtle pastels, and bring on the moss phlox! This is the phlox that jumps out at us with its bright flowers in early spring as we drive by a garden at 50 mph. Wherever it grows, moss phlox gets noticed.

Top Reasons to Plant

○ Bright spring flowers
○ Easy to grow
○ Spreads rapidly
○ Evergreen foliage
○ Few pests and diseases
○ Drought tolerant

Useful Hint

To make sure you get the colors you want, buy moss phlox when it's already in bloom.

Bloom Color
Red-purple, violet-purple, lavender, pink, or white

Bloom Period
Early to midspring

Height/Width
3 to 6 inches x 12 inches

Planting Location
- Well-drained, average garden soil with coarse sand or other gritty material added to heavy soils to improve drainage
- Sun

Planting
- Set out plants spring through summer.
- Space plants 12 inches apart.
- Water well.

Watering
- During hot summer weather, provide an inch of water each week if there hasn't been that much rainfall.

Fertilizing
- No fertilizer is needed.

Suggestions for Vigorous Growth
- Prune back foliage after the bloom is over.

Easy Tip

If you really want to create a bold statement, plant moss phlox of each different color all massed together.

Pest Control
- Spider mites may appear in dry weather—prevent them by occasionally spraying the foliage.

Complementary Plants
- Use as ground cover for early-blooming bulbs, such as lavender crocus or dwarf daffodils.
- Plant on a steep, sunny slope or in a rock garden for excellent effect.
- Plant in the crevices of rock walls if there's some soil to grab onto.

Recommended Selections
- 'Oakington Blue Eyes' has sky-blue flowers.
- 'White Delight' has large white flowers.
- *Phlox stolonifera* is a good creeping phlox for shade gardens, flowering in a range of colors including white, pink, violet, and blue.

Moss Rose

Portulaca grandiflora

A Tough Little Annual That's Bright and Carefree

Moss rose offers Georgia gardeners colorful blooms for hot, dry spots where few other flowers survive. Native to Brazil, this succulent grows happily along the Georgia coast and throughout the state as long as it gets lots of sun and heat. With their fleshy, needlelike leaves, these plants resemble moss plants when they clump together. This prostrate creeper makes a bright carpet of dazzling, 1-inch-wide satiny flowers.

Top Reasons to Plant

- Thrives in hot, dry, sunny locations
- Bright, showy blooms in many colors
- Good in hanging baskets or window boxes
- Easy to grow
- Needs no grooming
- Attracts few pests
- Newer types have flowers staying open all day

Bloom Color
White, bright shades of red, yellow, orange, rose, or purple

Bloom Period
Summer to frost

Height/Width
6 to 8 inches x 12 to 24 inches

Planting Location
- Well-drained, not-too-rich soil, with coarse soil added to heavier soils
- Full sun
- In containers, with "sharp" sand added to potting mix

Planting
- Start seeds indoors in a warm spot about six to eight weeks before the last frost date.
- Set plants out several weeks after the last frost, when the weather has settled and become warm.
- *Or* purchase bedding plants for the garden and for hanging baskets.
- *Or* sow seeds directly in the garden where the plants are to grow after the soil has warmed up.
- Do not mulch; the sun must warm the soil.

Watering
- Once plants are established, they shouldn't need watering except during periods of drought.

Easy Tip
Moss rose makes a good ground cover on a sunny bank with bright flowers from early summer until frost.

Fertilizing
- No fertilizer is needed.

Suggestions for Vigorous Growth
- Allow moss rose to thrive in warm soil and sun.
- Don't overwater.

Pest Control
- No serious pests or diseases trouble this plant.

Complementary Plants
- Use in rock gardens or along sidewalks and driveways.
- Plant as a filler next to perennials that only bloom for a short time.
- Combine with other succulents, such as sedums and hardy cactuses, or with ornamental grasses.

Recommended Selections
- Sundial series hybrids bloom earlier than other types, and the double flowers come in many colors.
- 'Afternoon Delight' offers many brightly colored flowers that stay open all day.
- 'Minilaca Mix' is a dwarf hybrid.
- 'Sunglo' offers long-blooming double flowers in ten shades.

Mottled Wild Ginger

Asarum shuttleworthii 'Callaway'

An Evergreen Perennial That Looks Good Year Round

Discovered at Callaway Gardens in Pine Mountain, Georgia, this vigorous selection of wild ginger has evergreen, heart-shaped, shiny green leaves with lighter cream markings. The leaves look something like those of hardy cyclamen. Planted in a woodland, in moist but well-drained soil, this selection of wild ginger forms evergreen clumps that look good year-round, even during the heat of our summers when other plants look wilted and worn out.

Top Reasons to Plant

- Good-looking foliage year-round
- Thrives in shade
- Elegant appearance
- Few pests and diseases
- Likes moist soils

Useful Hint

'Callaway' is an evergreen, but it's not fast-spreading like ivy or vinca, so it's perhaps best used as a specimen plant.

Bloom Color
Purple-brown, not showy

Bloom Period
Early spring

Height/Width
2 feet x 2 feet

Planting Location
• Rich, well-drained soil with lots of organic matter and no competition from tree roots
• Shade or part shade

Planting
• Set out plants in spring or early fall.
• Space plants 18 to 24 inches apart.
• Water well.
• Mulch well.

Watering
• Provide an inch of water each week that there isn't that much rainfall.

Fertilizing
• No fertilizer is needed.

Suggestions for Vigorous Growth
• Apply a layer of organic mulch in spring and fall.
• Keep well watered—if soil stays too dry, plants will look wilted and unattractive.

Easy Tip

Children will have fun discovering "little brown jugs," the inconspicuous flowers hidden beneath the leaves of wild ginger.

Pest Control
• No serious pests or diseases trouble this plant.

Complementary Plants
• For a tapestry effect, plant wild ginger with more aggressive ground covers such as ajuga or foamflower.
• For an excellent effect, plant with other woodland species such as ferns and hellebores.
• Use with spring-blooming woodland phlox and small bulbs such as dwarf iris.

Recommended Selections
• Canadian wild ginger (*Asarum canadense*) has broad, heart-shaped leaves up to 7 inches across; it grows 6 to 12 inches high—it's not evergreen but tolerates our extreme heat.

New Guinea Impatiens

Impatiens hawkeri

A Glamorous Annual Impatiens That Shows Off in the Sun

The flowers of impatiens and New Guinea impatiens are somewhat similar, but that is where the likeness ends. New Guineas are grown mostly for their jazzy, variegated foliage and the showy colors of their flowers. It's ideal where you want a plant that creates a festive feeling and calls attention to itself—near the swimming pool, for instance. Unlike *Impatiens walleriana*, New Guinea impatiens, introduced into this country in the 1970s, are not shade plants.

Top Reasons to Plant

- Tropical look
- Striking variegated foliage
- Large flowers in showy colors
- Likes mostly sun
- Few pests and diseases
- Great in containers near the pool or deck
- Attracts hummingbirds

Useful Hint

New Guinea impatiens like a bit of afternoon shade, but they do best in mostly sunny spots.

76

Bloom Color
White, red, pink, or salmon with leaves that are green or red-bronze, some variegated with creamy yellow

Bloom Period
Summer to first frost

Height/Width
12 to 20 inches x 12 to 15 inches

Planting Location
- Good garden soil enriched with plenty of organic matter
- Full sun or a few hours of late-afternoon shade
- Large (3-gallon) tubs or containers filled with a peat-based potting mix with rotted compost added

Planting
- Set plants out after all danger of frost has passed.
- Space plants 12 to 15 inches apart in the garden.
- Use 3 plants per 3-gallon container.
- Water well using a water-soluble root stimulator.
- Mulch well.

Watering
- Keep well watered.

Fertilizing
- Water with water-soluble fertilizer, such as 20-20-20, every other week, alternating with 10-56-0.
- If leaves turn pale or yellow (unless they're supposed to be yellow), fertilize the plant more often.

Easy Tip
The variety 'Tango Improved' may be grown from seed started indoors a few weeks before the last frost.

Suggestions for Vigorous Growth
- Pinch out plant tops once when they are 4 inches tall.
- Pinch thereafter as needed to keep a bushy shape.
- Flowers fall off on their own, so no deadheading is needed.

Pest Control
- Few insects or diseases bother New Guineas, except for spider mites in dry conditions.
- Spray water on leaves at least weekly to prevent spider mites.

Complementary Plants
- For an instant trip to the tropics, plant New Guineas with canna and agapanthus.
- Use New Guineas as a bridge between blooms in a sunny perennial bed.

Recommended Selections
- 'Tonga' has bronze and green leaves with lavender and purple flowers.

Pansy
Viola × wittrockiana

A Cheerful Little Annual to Brighten the Winter

In Georgia, particularly in the middle and northern parts of the state, pansies are popular for the flower garden or for containers. Planted in fall, they bloom for months during the winter, their colorful faces providing cheer on all but the coldest of days. Even when plants look shriveled and wilted from extreme cold, with just a bit of warmth and sunshine, they're quick to recover and continue blooming until well into spring.

Top Reasons to Plant

○ Flowers during winter
○ Perky little blooms
○ Wide range of colors
○ Excellent interplanted with spring bulbs
○ Good in containers
○ Nice cut flowers in small vases
○ Will lure you out of doors in winter

Useful Hint

Pansies won't bloom during winter's coldest weather, but the flowers return quickly during warm spells.

Bloom Color
Red, yellow, orange, blue, violet, and white, both single colors and bicolors, many with "faces"

Bloom Period
Fall to spring

Height/Width
4 to 8 inches x 4 to 8 inches

Planting Location
- Well-drained, cool, moist soil rich in organic matter
- Sun in winter and partial shade in spring

Planting
- Set out plants in early fall—the sooner they're planted, the more their roots grow, and the hardier they are.
- Space the plants no more than 3 inches apart—they won't grow and fill in over winter, which is when you want the show.
- Water well with a root stimulator.
- Mulch.

Watering
- Pansies require consistent moisture, so they may need watering several times a week in windy weather.

Fertilizing
- Use a water-soluble fertilizer for blooming plants once a month until the ground freezes and again in spring.
- During winter thaws, fertilize again.

Suggestions for Vigorous Growth
- For fuller, healthier plants, pinch off the flower buds when you first plant them.

Easy Tip
Once the plants are established, mulch to protect roots and prevent them from being heaved out of the ground by frost.

- Keep old flowers trimmed off to extend the bloom season.

Pest Control
- If plants get leggy or suffer from stem rot, leaf spots, or anthracnose, just cut them back, and they'll put out new growth.

Complementary Plants
- For an elegant carpet, plant pansies in coordinating colors over your daffodils and tulips.

Recommended Selections
- The Crystal Bowl series is a clear-faced, early-flowering type that grows 8 inches tall with 2-inch blooms.
- Antique Shades have flowers in soft pastel colors.
- Bird's foot violet (*Viola pedata*), a hardy perennial native to Georgia, requires a well-drained soil and is found naturally along road cuts or rock outcroppings.
- Johnny-jump-up (*Viola tricolor*) often reseeds itself and delights us by showing up in unexpected places.

Pentas

Pentas lanceolata

A Lush Annual That Gives the Garden a Tropical Flair

In our current rush to grow lush-looking tropical plants, pentas is finally starting to get the attention it deserves. That's because it's easy to grow, doesn't mind the steamiest summer, and blooms for a long time. Besides, it's pretty. The round flower clusters—consisting of dozens of tiny, star-shaped blossoms (giving rise to the common names star flower and Egyptian star cluster)—are often red or pink, adding to the "hot" look.

Top Reasons to Plant

- Tropical-looking clusters of blossoms
- Attracts butterflies and hummingbirds
- Thrives on heat and humidity
- Easy to grow
- Long bloom period
- Good in containers
- Few pests and diseases

Useful Hint

Pentas draws butterflies to your yard like a magnet.

Bloom Color
Pink, rose, purple, or white

Bloom Period
Summer

Height/Width
14 to 24 inches x 10 to 14 inches

Planting Location
- Well-drained, very rich soil containing plenty of compost and ground bark or rotted sawdust if drainage is a particular problem
- Sun

Planting
- Pentas is widely available at nurseries, but if you want to grow it from seed, sow seeds indoors in a cool (60 degrees Fahrenheit) environment ten weeks before the last frost.
- Set plants out about three weeks after the last frost, when the soil has warmed.
- Work a pelleted, slow-release fertilizer into the soil.
- Space plants 6 to 8 inches apart.
- Water well after planting.
- Mulch generously.

Watering
- Pentas likes abundant moisture, so water several times a week in dry weather.
- Water container-grown pentas often to ensure that the plants don't wilt.

Fertilizing
- Fertilize between blooming periods with a water-soluble plant food made for flowering plants.

Easy Tip
Mulch heavily to reduce the need to water.

Suggestions for Vigorous Growth
- Keep spent flowers picked off.
- Pinch young plants once to encourage bushy plants with multiple flower heads.
- As plants grow, pinch to maintain shape.
- Cuttings root easily in potting soil all summer.
- If pentas gets starved and thirsty, it will grow woody—cut the plant back, and it may rejuvenate itself.

Pest Control
- Slugs may eat pentas but they will eat other plants first.

Complementary Plants
- Combine with petunia, asparagus fern, and purple fountain grass in a huge urn for a special patio centerpiece.

Recommended Selections
- 'Pink Profusion' has a pretty color.
- 'Ruby Glow' is good with yellow coreopsis.

Petunia

Petunia × hybrida

An Updated Annual Offering Lots of Variety

For bright color all summer, petunias are unsurpassed. We now have a number of varieties to choose from that don't need deadheading, and the flowers hold up in our heat, humidity, and rain. The low-spreading 'Purple Wave' grows only 6 inches tall, and its rose-purple, 3-inch blooms cascade or spread up to 5 feet. *Petunia integrifolia* has tiny, ¹/₂- to 1-inch magenta blooms with deep violet centers and small foliage, making it ideal for containers of all sorts.

Top Reasons to Plant

- Beautiful, classic summer flower
- Wide range of colors
- Long bloom season
- Excellent in containers
- Attracts hummingbirds and butterflies
- Fragrant flowers

Useful Hint

While large grandiflora petunias are glitzy, the single multifloras aren't beaten down by rain, which is a valuable quality.

Bloom Color
White or every shade of rose, red, pink, purple, yellow, or bicolors

Bloom Period
Summer until frost

Height/Width
6 to 18 inches x 12 to 24 inches

Planting Location
- Light, well-drained soil
- Sun to partial shade; petunias can grow in full sun if they have lots of water, but they appreciate an hour or two of afternoon shade and also grow with a half day's sun.

Planting
- Set out plants after all danger of frost has passed and on into midsummer.
- Space plants according to mature size.
- Mix a pelleted, slow-release fertilizer into the soil.
- Mulch lightly to moderate soil conditions.

Watering
- Water often to keep the bed or container from drying out.

Fertilizing
- Use a water-soluble fertilizer for flowering plants once a month.

Suggestions for Vigorous Growth
- Pinch stems after the first flowers appear to encourage bushy plants and more blooms.
- Shear back leggy plants and fertilize to rejuvenate.

Easy Tip
To avoid having to pick off spent blooms, be sure to get a type of petunia that doesn't require deadheading to keep blooming.

Pest Control
- Whiteflies may be a problem in overly dry conditions.
- Botrytis and Pythium rots may occur in overly damp conditions.
- Consult the Extension Service about remedies.

Complementary Plants
- Use hybrids such as 'Purple Wave' as ground cover.
- Place wherever in the garden you want a spot of bright, summer color.

Recommended Selections
- 'The Pearl' has single, fragrant, 2-inch flowers that hold up to weather extremes and bloom all summer.
- In addition to 'Purple Wave', look for 'Saul's Pink Wave'.
- 'Lavender Storm' was developed for its rain-resistant lavender flowers that are 3 inches wide on 12-inch plants.

Purple Coneflower

Echinacea purpurea

A Wonderful Perennial That Requires No Care

Purple coneflower is a tough native that performs well for Georgia gardeners. Blooming for a long period in the summer, it resembles black-eyed Susan except for its purple petals. A perennial favorite of butterflies for its nectar and of flower arrangers for its blossoms and dried cone heads, purple coneflower is an easy-care flower for the garden or the meadow.

Top Reasons to Plant

- Long bloom season
- Likes poor soil
- Drought tolerant
- Beautiful, drooping daisylike flowers
- Attracts butterflies
- Good cut flower
- Easy to grow
- Few pests and diseases
- Excellent in naturalized settings

Useful Hint

If you want to make a dried arrangement, cut purple coneflowers early when the coneheads are still tight.

84

Bloom Color
Purple with orange-brown cones in center

Bloom Period
Summer

Height/Width
4 feet x 1 to 2 feet

Planting Location
- Well-drained soil not rich in organic matter
- Sun

Planting
- Plant in spring or fall.
- Space clumps 18 to 24 inches apart.
- Do not bury the crown (the point where roots and stems meet) when planting.
- Mulch up to but not over the crown.

Watering
- Water deeply but infrequently to encourage deep roots and drought resistance.

Fertilizing
- No fertilizer is needed except for a light dressing of compost in spring.
- Too much fertilizer results in tall stems and fewer flowers.

Suggestions for Vigorous Growth
- Keep early faded flowers picked off to encourage bloom.
- Leave the last blooms intact so the seedheads will attract birds.
- Divide plants every four years.

Easy Tip
Leave the last round of flowers on the plants to produce seeds for the birds and to provide more plants.

Pest Control
- Japanese beetles may be a problem; pick off small infestations, and drown the beetles in a jar of water or oil.
- Leaf spot may appear—check with your Extension Agent about controls.

Complementary Plants
- Put purple coneflowers in the middle or back of a border beside finer-textured perennials and annuals, such as *Artemisia* 'Powis Castle'.
- Plant in butterfly gardens with butterfly bushes and coreopsis.

Recommended Selections
- 'Bright Star' grows to 2 to 3 feet and has bright, rose-red flowers with maroon centers.
- White selections include 'White Lustre', a good bloomer even in dry areas, and 'White Swan', a good cut flower.

Purple Heart

Tradescantia purpurea 'Purple Heart'

An Annual That Shows Off in the Garden

The deep-purple foliage of purple heart stands out in the garden. The challenge is where to plant this not-so-subtle showman. A low-maintenance plant, purple heart thrives in all types of soils from clay to sandy, providing they're well-drained. This persistent plant tolerates salt spray, making it a good choice for coastal gardens. One option is to grow it in a container that can serve as a focal point in the garden and move it around as needed.

Top Reasons to Plant

○ Showy purple foliage
○ Adapts to variety of soils
○ Tolerates salt spray
○ Good focal point
○ Excellent in hanging baskets and window boxes
○ Easy to grow
○ No pests or diseases

Useful Hint

Purple heart overwinters in much of the state, losing its foliage in cold weather but returning with new growth in spring.

Bloom Color
Violet-purple

Bloom Period
Spring to fall

Height/Width
12 inches x 12 to 24 inches

Planting Location
• Well-drained soil either clay or sand
• Sun or partial shade

Planting
• Set out plants in spring or early fall.
• Space plants 12 to 18 inches apart.
• Water well.

Watering
• Water deeply during drought.

Fertilizing
• No fertilizer is needed.

Suggestions for Vigorous Growth
• Do not plant in soggy soils—the plants will rot.

Pest Control
• No serious pests or diseases trouble this plant.

Easy Tip

Purple heart roots easily—if you cut back the tips and stick the cuttings in the ground, you'll have rooted plants in about two weeks.

Complementary Plants
• Plant in a border with reds and other purples.
• Combine with gray and silver foliage plants.
• Use effectively as a ground cover for a sandy slope.

Recommended Selections
• A close relative is the spiderwort (*Tradescantia* x *andersoniana*), which is considered weedy by some but grows in sun or shade and tolerates moist to soggy soils, unlike purple heart; the flowers are violet-purple, white, pink, or red and are larger than those of purple heart.

Sedum 'Autumn Joy'

Hylotelephium 'Autumn Joy' ('Herbstfreude')

A Valuable Perennial Interesting in All Growing Seasons

This is a great plant for gardeners who claim they "don't have a green thumb." All it needs to thrive is sun or light shade and any soil that's well-drained. In early spring, 'Autumn Joy' sends up gray-green buds. In midsummer, the flat-topped flower heads look like broccoli. As summer progresses, the flower buds turn pink and finally deep rose. Showy late into the fall, these flowers dry on their stems, turning rust as they age.

Top Reasons to Plant

- Interesting foliage all summer
- Blooms that change color as they age
- Attracts butterflies
- Doesn't need fertilizer
- Cuttings root easily
- Good cut flower
- Fall blooms when few perennials have blossoms

Useful Hint

Perfect for creating interest in the winter garden, the dried flower stalks of 'Autumn Joy' last until spring—cut them back in early spring.

Bloom Color
Pink or reddish shades, maturing to darker colors

Bloom Period
Late summer to fall

Height/Width
12 to 24 inches x 12 to 24 inches

Planting Location
- Well-drained garden soil that isn't overly fertile
- Sun or light shade

Planting
- Set plants out from late spring until early fall.
- Space plants 12 to 24 inches apart.
- Mulch lightly or not at all.

Watering
- Water regularly but moderately in weeks with less than an inch of rain.
- Allow the soil to dry out between waterings.
- Shallow root systems cannot take large amounts of water when small.

Fertilizing
- Do not fertilize.

Suggestions for Vigorous Growth
- Pinch out the tips of 'Autumn Joy' once in late spring and again in early summer to encourage bushiness and to keep it compact.
- If plants located in partial sun flop over, cut them back to about 12 inches tall in late June to keep plants bushy and full.

Easy Tip
Left undisturbed, 'Autumn Joy' grows and blooms for years without any special care, and it can also be easily propagated by division.

- Space correctly when planting and these plants won't need dividing for many years.
- If clumps become open in center due to too much shade or overly fertile soil, divide and transplant the clumps in spring.

Pest Control
- Few pests or diseases bother 'Autumn Joy'.

Complementary Plants
- 'Autumn Joy' looks good with other sedums including ground cover types— *Sedum kamtschaticum* grows 4 to 6 inches tall with yellow flowers in summer; *Sedum ternatum* grows 2 to 6 inches tall with white flowers in spring.
- Plant in combination with ornamental grasses and other perennials such as black-eyed Susan.

Recommended Selections
- *Sedum sieboldii* grows 6 to 8 inches tall with blue-green leaves and pink flowers in late summer to early autumn.

Snapdragon

Antirrhinum majus

A Colorful Annual with Blooms Beloved by Children Everywhere

Snaps are favorites of many gardeners, and not only because of their childhood memories of snapping the hinged flowers to make them look as if they are talking. Individual flowers open over two weeks, starting at the bottom of the spike and continuing upward. Young plants set out in the fall will bloom until a hard frost. Then they rest over the winter and start blooming again in early spring. In the warmest parts of Georgia, snapdragons act like perennials, and in the rest of the state, they'll bloom off and on during mild spells in the winter.

Top Reasons to Plant

- Bountiful stalks of flowers with a unique shape
- Great cut flower
- Perennial at annual prices
- Wide range of colors—everything except blue
- Long blooming season
- Good selection of heights for all purposes
- Attracts butterflies and hummingbirds

Useful Hint

Cut snapdragons for arrangements when one-third of the flowers on a stem are open.

Bloom Color
Pink, red, purple, yellow, or white in solids and bicolors

Bloom Period
Early spring until frost

Height/Width
6 to 36 inches x 12 inches

Planting Location
- Well-drained soil
- Sun to light shade

Planting
- Set out plants in spring or fall.
- Space plants based on their mature size.
- Plant in containers using a peat-based or soilless potting mix.
- Mix pelleted, slow-release fertilizer into the soil.
- Water well with a root stimulator.

Watering
- Water frequently until plants become established.
- Water established plants enough that they don't dry out.

Fertilizing
- Use a water-soluble fertilizer for blooming plants.

Suggestions for Vigorous Growth
- When plants stop blooming in the summer heat, cut them back by one-third and keep them watered.
- Once plants begin growing again, resume fertilizing for fall flowers.
- Deadhead regularly to keep plants blooming.

Easy Tip

Let some plants set seed, and snapdragons will sow themselves around the garden, creating some interesting color combinations.

Pest Control
- Rust can be a problem.
- Look for rust-resistant varieties, use soaker hoses to water, and leave space between plants for air circulation.

Complementary Plants
- Mix yellow snapdragons with variegated *Liriope* or purple-flowered *Verbena bonariensis*.
- Snapdragons make a nice complement to pansies in the garden or in containers.

Recommended Selections
- The Rocket series grows 30 to 36 inches and comes in over ten different colors—it's great for cut flowers.
- The Tahiti series is one of the earliest snapdragons to flower and is very compact, growing to only 7 to 8 inches tall.

Spider Flower
Cleome hassleriana

A Lovely Old-Fashioned Annual That Beats the Heat

Whether you call it spider flower, cat's whiskers, or needle and thread, this vigorous plant has unusual blooms with stamens that stick out way past the petals. The large rounded heads of flowers come in shades of pink, pink and white, lavender, and white. The pure white form works in every type of color scheme. And spider flower grows almost anywhere that's hot, humid, and sunny, reseeding itself freely.

Top Reasons to Plant

○ Tall, graceful blooms
○ Unusual flower shape
○ Withstands heat and humidity
○ Self-seeds readily
○ Easy to grow
○ Has few pests or diseases
○ Fragrant
○ Attracts butterflies and hummingbirds

Useful Hint

During the dog days of summer and continuing until frost, few annuals can match the spider flower's height, texture, and color.

Bloom Color
Pink, white, purple, or lavender

Bloom Period
Summer until frost

Height/Width
4 to 6 feet x 1 to 1$^1/_2$ feet

Planting Location
• Average, well-drained soil
• Sun
• Out of the wind

Planting
• Refrigerate cleome seeds during winter, then plant after the last expected frost.
• *Or* sow seeds indoors in a warm environment six to eight weeks before the last expected frost.
• Thin or set plants 18 to 24 inches apart.
• Fertilize plants with a root stimulator and mix a pelleted, slow-release fertilizer into the soil.
• Water plants well.
• Mulch lightly to permit cleome to reseed.

Watering
• Water often enough to prevent wilting; once dried out, cleome may not grow or bloom well.

Fertilizing
• Fertilize monthly with a water-soluble plant food, such as 20-20-20.

Suggestions for Vigorous Growth
• When plants are a foot tall, pinch an inch off the tip of the main stem to encourage branching.

Easy Tip

Let some of the flowers set seeds and self-sow—just pull up any plants you don't want.

Pest Control
• If aphids appear, spray with insecticidal soap.
• If leaf spot develops, pick off the affected leaves and dispose of them.

Complementary Plants
• Plant a group of cleomes in the middle or at the back of a flower bed with low-growing annuals such as the white-flowered form of *Zinnia linearis* in front to mask cleome's bare stems.
• For a nice look, plant cleome with silver-leafed artemisia at its base.

Recommended Selections
• 'Helen Campbell', which grows about 4 feet tall, has glossy white flowers.
• The Queen series plants grow 4 feet tall with flower heads that are 5 to 6 inches wide—colors range from cherry to pink, rose, violet, and white.

Sunflower

Helianthus annuus

A Classic Summer Annual with Lots of Brand-New Looks

Gardeners and artists alike have long been inspired by sunflowers. There's nothing quite so magical as a huge field of these tall flowers with cheerful yellow faces that follow the sun. Upon close examination, each face is unique and charming. Sunflowers are easy to grow, and with the many hybrids available today, the flowers range from dainty 1-inch blooms to the 'Mammoth Russian', which quickly grows to 12 feet tall.

Top Reasons to Plant

○ Bright summery blooms
○ Wide range of colors
○ Heights from 2 feet to mammoth
○ Beloved by children and birds
○ Good cut flower
○ Easy to grow
○ Drought tolerant when established
○ Few pests and diseases

Useful Hint

Let late flowers set seed for the birds or for you to store for next year's crop.

Bloom Color
Cream, yellow, burgundy, orange

Bloom Period
Summer

Height/Width
24 inches to 12 feet x 12 to 24 inches

Planting Location
- Best in well-drained, moist soil enriched with organic matter
- Full sun

Planting
- Sunflowers don't always transplant well, so plant seeds outdoors where you want them to grow.
- Sow seeds after danger of frost has passed and soil is warm.
- Starting seeds of different types every few weeks will extend the period of bloom over the summer.
- Mix a handful of 6-12-12 fertilizer into prepared soil.
- Keep the soil moist until seeds sprout.
- Thin plants to 1 to 4 feet apart, depending on their mature size.

Watering
- These drought-tolerant plants require little water once established, but regular water will produce bigger and better blooms.

Fertilizing
- In midsummer, spread a handful of 6-12-12 in a circle 6 to 12 inches away from the stem.
- Water dry fertilizer in well.

Easy Tip
If you plant sunflowers in too much shade, they'll lean toward the light and require staking.

Suggestions for Vigorous Growth
- Many of the new types have multiple flower heads and bloom longer if deadheaded.

Pest Control
- Sunflowers have few pest and disease problems.

Complementary Plants
- Plant shorter types with butterfly weed, coreopsis, and gaillardia.
- Plant tall types against a dark background, such as a fence or a row of evergreens.
- Use large types to create a screen or a background for other plants.

Recommended Selections
- 'Sonja' has deep-tangerine-orange flowers on $3^1/_2$-foot stems.
- "Large Flowered Mix" produces flowers of red, yellow, and bronze that are 6 inches across on 10-foot stems.

Sweet Alyssum

Lobularia maritima

A Pretty Low-Growing Annual with a Fabulous Scent

Seeing—and smelling—sweet alyssum transports you back to a quieter, slower time. This sweet little plant, covered with tiny blooms and giving off a delightful fragrance, has a wonderfully old-fashioned feel. It reminds you of your grandmother's garden, but will be right at home in yours—if you have a sunny spot in reach of the hose. Low-growing sweet alyssum brings the best of the past to the present.

Top Reasons to Plant

- Lots of tiny, showy flowers
- Wonderful fragrance
- Low growing
- Attracts butterflies
- Easy to grow
- Few pests and diseases

Useful Hint

The white-flowered varieties of sweet alyssum mix well with everything and provide a fresh, clean look.

Bloom Color
White, purple, pink, or light salmon

Bloom Period
Spring to frost

Height/Width
3 to 6 inches x 12 to 18 inches

Planting Location
- Good garden soil amended with compost if the natural soil has clay or sand
- Sun or a little shade

Planting
- Sow seeds directly into the garden three weeks before the last expected frost.
- Purchase plants at any garden center.
- Work a pelleted, slow-release fertilizer into the soil before planting.
- Thin seedlings to 4 inches apart when they're an inch tall.
- Set purchased plants 6 to 8 inches apart.
- Water well.

Watering
- Water before the soil dries out completely.

Fertilizing
- Every two or three weeks, feed with a water-soluble fertilizer such as 20-20-20.

Suggestions for Vigorous Growth
- Once plants are established, mulch to help moderate soil conditions and retain moisture.
- To help sweet alyssum tolerate drought better, plant in light to medium shade.

Easy Tip
Scatter a few seeds between cracks in sidewalks or spaces between flagstones, or in rock walls—sweet alyssum loves warm concrete and stone.

- If plants go dormant in the hottest part of summer, shear them back to rejuvenate them.
- This plant reseeds but is not invasive—pull extra seedlings out; they won't resprout.

Pest Control
- Few pests bother sweet alyssum except occasional caterpillar larvae that usually cause little damage.

Complementary Plants
- Plant beneath roses with artemisia for a cottage-garden look.

Recommended Selections
- Deep pink 'Rosie O'Day' is very fragrant—a true edger, it grows only 3 inches tall.
- 'Snow Crystals', which is white and about 6 inches tall, is very heat-tolerant.

Tartarian Daisy

Aster tartaricus

A Perennial Daisy Always Welcome in the Fall

After the dog days of summer, the fall garden can delight us with its brilliant foliage and flowers. The Tartarian daisy grows happily in Georgia gardens in full sun or part shade. Tough and adaptable, this perennial comes into bloom in late autumn just when many plants have packed up for the season. After only one year, the slender but strong flower stalks can reach up to 7 feet.

Top Reasons to Plant

○ Masses of lavender daisies
○ Blooms in fall
○ Tolerates heat and humidity
○ Vigorous grower
○ Needs little care
○ Few pests or diseases
○ Good cut flower

Useful Hint

If you don't want Tartarian daisy to grow so vigorously, plant it in a dry spot.

Bloom Color
Lavender

Bloom Period
September to November

Height/Width
6 to 7 feet x 2 to 4 feet

Planting Location
• Prefers moist, average soil but will grow—more slowly—in dry soil
• Sun or partial shade

Planting
• Set plants out in early spring or fall.
• Space plants 2 to 4 feet apart.
• Water well.

Watering
• Regular watering during drought produces faster, larger growth.

Fertilizing
• No fertilizer is needed.

Suggestions for Vigorous Growth
• Divide clumps every few years if the aster spreads too much.

Pest Control
• No serious pests or diseases trouble this plant.

Easy Tip

Plant this aster at the back of the border where it can lean over flowers that bloom earlier in the season.

Complementary Plants
• Mix with *Callicarpa americana*, whose purple fruits make a striking display with Tartarian aster's lavender flowers.
• Combine with Joe-pye weed and goldenrod, especially *Solidago rugosa* 'Fireworks', which blooms for weeks.

Recommended Selections
• Another favorite fall-blooming aster is *Aster novae-angliae* 'Harrington's Pink', which grows 3 to 5 feet tall and has salmon-pink flowers.
• 'Hella Lacy' has violet-blue daisies on 4- to 5-foot-tall plants.
• *Aster lateriflorus* 'Prince' has deep-purple foliage and white daisies.

Threadleaf Coreopsis
Coreopsis verticillata

A Wonderful Perennial with Fine Foliage and Lovely Blossoms

Many types of coreopsis, both annual and perennial, grow in the wild, brightening spring and summer with their yellow-orange flowers. One of the best perennials for the garden is *Coreopsis verticillata*, whose common name, threadleaf coreopsis, describes its foliage texture—finely cut leaves that give the plant a ferny look. One of the most popular cultivars, 'Moonbeam', grows 18 to 24 inches tall and has pale-yellow, daisylike flowers from June to October.

Top Reasons to Plant

○ Dainty appearance
○ Lovely flowers
○ Long season of bloom
○ Few pests and diseases
○ Easy to grow

Useful Hint

'Moonbeam' is not the best choice in the hottest parts of the state—the flowers are short-lived and the plants never look happy.

100

Bloom Color
Pale-yellow to bright-yellow or deep-red

Bloom Period
Late spring to late summer

Height/Width
18 to 36 inches x 18 to 24 inches

Planting Location
- Moderately fertile, well-drained soil, including sandy soil
- Sun or light afternoon shade

Planting
- Set out plants in spring or fall.
- Space plants according to mature height.
- Water well with a transplanting solution.
- Mulch well.

Watering
- Provide an inch of water each week if there isn't that amount of rainfall.

Fertilizing
- The first spring after planting, feed with a balanced fertilizer such as 10-10-10.

Suggestions for Vigorous Growth
- After the flowers stop blooming, cut back the flowering stems to encourage a new crop of leaves and more blooms.

Pest Control
- No serious pests or diseases trouble this plant.

Easy Tip
Coreopsis rosea can become an invasive weed in the warmest parts of Georgia, so it's best to choose another cultivar for those areas.

Complementary Plants
- *Coreopsis verticillata* 'Moonbeam' looks good with the electric-blue flowers of hardy plumbago (*Ceratostigma plumbaginoides*), as well as with the daylily 'Happy Returns', which blooms in a similar creamy-yellow.
- Any of the cultivars are effective next to perennials with bold foliage, such as lamb's ears and purple coneflowers, or spiky flowers such as salvias.

Recommended Selections
- 'Moonbeam' has soft-yellow flowers that blend with everything.
- 'Golden Showers' has larger and louder blooms with its 2$\frac{1}{2}$-inch golden-yellow flowers.
- 'Zagreb' is more compact, growing to 18 inches, and has flowers that are deeper yellow than those of 'Moonbeam'.
- 'Limerock Ruby' has deep-red flowers and grows to 18 to 24 inches.
- *Coreopsis rosea*, a pink-flowered form, has a growth habit similar to that of 'Moonbeam'.

Verbena
Verbena 'Homestead Purple'

A Georgia Perennial That Looks Good All Season

Verbena 'Homestead Purple' was discovered growing in a patch of weeds on the side of a road in Georgia by Drs. Michael Dirr and Allan Armitage, two well-known plantsmen and professors at the University of Georgia. The large clusters of velvety rich-purple flowers bloom on and off from May until frost, and the mildew-resistant foliage, dark-green above and gray-green below, looks good all season.

Top Reasons to Plant

○ Tolerates sandy soil
○ Drought tolerant
○ Long season of bloom
○ Reseeds easily
○ Few pests or diseases
○ Good cut flower
○ Attracts butterflies

Useful Hint

Even if the foliage of 'Homestead Purple' is killed back in winter, its roots survive and put out new growth in spring.

Bloom Color
Purple

Bloom Period
Summer to fall

Height/Width
10 inches x 2 to 3 feet

Planting Location
- Well-drained, moderately fertile soil
- Sun
- Containers

Planting
- Set out plants in spring or early fall so they have plenty of time to get established before winter.
- Space plants two to three feet apart—plant 'Homestead Purple' where it can creep around at will.
- Water well.
- Mulch but do not cover the plants' crowns.

Watering
- Provide an inch of water in weeks without that amount of rainfall.

Fertilizing
- No fertilizer is needed—too much fertilizer or too rich a soil results in a lot of foliage and few blooms.

Suggestions for Vigorous Growth
- Do not cut back in fall—it survives winter better with more leaf surface.
- Mulch lightly in fall.

Easy Tip

'Homestead Purple' is evergreen and perennial except in the very coldest parts of the state.

- Be sure soil doesn't stay wet in winter.
- To encourage bushiness, cut back hard in spring once new growth has started.
- Propagate new plants every few years by digging up divisions that have taken root and transplanting them to new spots.

Pest Control
- No serious pests or diseases trouble this plant.

Complementary Plants
- Plant with purple sweet potato vine in hanging baskets and containers.
- Use with artemisias, lamb's ears, salvias, purple coneflowers, and daisies.
- For an excellent effect, plant as a carpet over early spring-flowering bulbs such as crocus.

Recommended Selections
- *Verbena tenuisecta* also creeps along the ground, but its lacy foliage has a much more graceful texture; it's better for coastal gardens—it isn't cold hardy and likes sandy, well-drained soils.

Wax Begonia

Begonia Semperflorens-Cultorum hybrids

A Versatile Annual That Grows Almost Anywhere

Native to Brazil, wax begonias have long been popular in the South as bedding plants in the shade garden, for edging, and for containers and window boxes. A profusion of flowers from spring until frost and the ability to thrive during the heat of Georgia summers make this annual popular with many people. Sun-resistant varieties include the Cocktail series, growing 5 to 6 inches high with colorful flowers that are especially showy against shiny bronze foliage.

Top Reasons to Plant

- Grows well in sun or shade
- Long season of bloom
- Neat edging plant
- Looks good in many settings
- Few serious insect or disease problems

Useful Hint

Avoid planting wax begonias directly under trees where there will be lots of competition for water and nutrients from the tree roots.

Bloom Color
White, pink, red, or bicolor

Bloom Period
Spring to frost

Height/Width
6 to 12 inches x 6 to 18 inches

Planting Location
- Soil that's rich in organic matter and stays consistently moist but not soggy
- Partial or full shade with no hot direct sun.

Planting
- Set plants out after threat of frost has passed.
- Add pelleted, slow-release fertilizer to soil at planting.
- Space plants 8 to 12 inches apart depending on mature size—extra-dwarf types should be planted 4 to 6 inches apart.
- Water well.
- Mulch abundantly.

Watering
- Keep well watered throughout the season.
- Wax begonias in containers may need watering twice a day during hot summer weather.

Fertilizing
- Twice monthly, apply a water-soluble fertilizer made for flowering plants.

Suggestions for Vigorous Growth
- Pinch tips back when plants are 4 inches tall to encourage branching and a fuller appearance.

Easy Tip
Wax begonias are sensitive to cold and cannot survive frost, but they're easy to overwinter as houseplants.

- If plants grow leggy, pinch tips back again.
- Cuttings root easily in water or potting soil.

Pest Control
- Few serious insect or disease problems bother wax begonia.
- Slugs may attack seedlings.
- Overwatering promotes root rot.
- In very dry conditions, whiteflies and spider mites may occur.
- Cut back plants, mulch, and water more often to prevent these insect pests.

Complementary Plants
- Mix plants among perennials in a shady bed to provide color in mid- to late summer, when perennials may have stopped blooming.

Recommended Selections
- The Pizzazz series grows 10 inches tall with waxy green leaves and is completely covered with deep-rose, pink, red, or white blossoms all summer.
- Stara series are vigorous plants that grow to 14 inches high.

Wild Indigo
Baptisia australis

A Native Perennial with Graceful Blue Flower Stalks

An adaptable native with handsome blue-green foliage and beautiful indigo-blue flowers, wild indigo is slow to become established, but after a few years, it should become a large clump. Left alone, it will thrive with little or no care. The inch-long, pealike flowers bloom on 10- to 12-inch stems for close to four weeks in spring. This easy-to-grow plant offers attractive foliage, beautiful flowers, and decorative seedpods.

Top Reasons to Plant

- Easy-care native plant
- Drought tolerant when established
- Attractive seedpods
- Beautiful bluish green foliage attractive after blooms fade
- Long spring-blooming season
- Attractive to butterflies and hummingbirds

Bloom Color
Blue

Bloom Period
Spring

Height/Width
3 to 5 feet x 4 to 5 feet

Planting Location
- Prefers rich, organic soil that drains well but tolerates poor soils with low fertility
- Full sun or partial shade

Planting
- Set out plants in spring or fall.
- Space plants 3 feet apart in their permanent location; once established, wild indigo is difficult to move successfully.
- Water well after planting.
- Mulch to keep soil cool.

Watering
- Water regularly to avoid wilting during the first year; after that, wild indigo tolerates drought.

Fertilizing
- Spread pelleted, slow-release fertilizer over the soil in spring.
- If leaves yellow prematurely during summer, use a water-soluble fertilizer for flowering plants that contains iron.

Useful Hint

Wild indigo is good planted in the middle or back of the flower border so its foliage can serve as a backdrop for other perennials.

Easy Tip

Wild indigo may take several years to produce many blooms, but once it's established in the garden, it will thrive for years with little or no care.

Suggestions for Vigorous Growth
- Young plants, or those in partial shade, may need staking.
- Cut off faded flowers to promote continuing bloom.
- Allow last flowers to go to seed—the seedpods are attractive and rustle in the breeze.
- Seed-grown plants may take up to five years to reach their full glory, so fertilize in spring to speed them along.

Pest Control
- Voles may be a problem, but otherwise wild indigo is generally very healthy.

Complementary Plants
- Plant with bearded iris, peonies, shasta daisies, black-eyed Susans, and cleome.

Recommended Selections
- *Baptisia alba* has white flowers in late spring but isn't as stately as *Baptisia australis*.
- *Baptisia tinctoria* has yellow flowers and blooms in summer.

Wishbone Flower

Torenia fournieri

Whether Clown or Wishbone, This Annual Enchants

The clown flower gets its name from its color—two-toned spotted flowers. Its other common name—wishbone flower—comes from the wishbone-shaped stamens found inside the flower's throat. Reminiscent of snapdragons, the $1^{1}/_{2}$-inch long tubular flowers are like small trumpets with a pronounced flare at the end. Both its flowers and seedpods look like tiny Chinese lanterns. This enchanting annual comes to us from Asia, but it loves our Southern climate.

Top Reasons to Plant

○ Attractive flowers
○ Long season of bloom
○ Thrives in heat and humidity
○ Requires little care
○ Few pests and diseases
○ Grows in sun or shade
○ Needs little care

Useful Hint

This old-fashioned plant with colorful flowers is a welcome alternative to the impatiens we see everywhere in Georgia gardens.

Bloom Color
Pale-lilac-blue with velvety dark-purple blotched bottom lip—throat interior marked with yellow

Bloom Period
Summer to frost

Height/Width
12 inches x 12 inches

Planting Location
- Prefers moist, moderately fertile soil
- Sun or shade
- Containers

Planting
- Sow seeds indoors in early spring or outdoors once the soil has warmed.
- Set plants out after all danger of frost has passed.
- Dig the hole as large as the plant's rootball.
- Set the plant at the same level it was growing previously.
- Firm the soil around the rootball.
- Water well.
- Mulch.

Watering
- Provide an inch of water each week that doesn't have that amount of rain.

Fertilizing
- For maximum bloom, feed monthly with a liquid fertilizer.

Easy Tip
Wishbone flower reseeds freely, providing plants for next year and years to come.

Suggestions for Vigorous Growth
- If plants become leggy, pinch them back—they'll quickly produce new growth.

Pest Control
- No serious pests or diseases trouble this plant.

Complementary Plants
- Use in a mass planting, or mix with other summer-bloomers.

Recommended Selections
- The Clown series offers flowers in blue, blue and white, burgundy, rose, violet, and a mixture.
- 'Compacta Blue' grows to 8 inches tall and has blue flowers with violet and yellow blotches on the lips.
- The Panda series has blue or pink flowers on plants 8 to 10 inches tall.
- *Torenia baillonii* 'Suzie Wong' grows to 8 inches with flowers that are intense yellow with a deep-purple-red, almost black, throat.

Zinnia

Zinnia linearis (angustifolia)

A Long-Blooming, Easy-Care Annual

One of the drawbacks to the ever popular common zinnias is that in our hot, humid weather, they're attacked by powdery mildew, which causes the foliage to look gray and unsightly. With *Zinnia linearis*, that doesn't happen. A much smaller plant with a spreading habit, the flowers look quite different than those most of us know as zinnias, but its vigor and long season of bloom make this gem worth seeking out.

Top Reasons to Plant

○ Healthy foliage
○ Bright, beautiful daisylike blooms
○ Tolerates heat and humidity
○ Spreading habit
○ Few pests and diseases
○ Good cut and dried flower

Useful Hint

Strains of the old-fashioned, large-flowered *Zinnia elegans* have been bred to resist powdery mildew—look for them if you want to plant traditional zinnias.

Bloom Color
Orange, yellow, or white

Bloom Period
Summer to frost

Height/Width
6 to 12 inches x 12 inches

Planting Location
- Moist, well-drained soil with lots of organic matter
- Sun
- Containers

Planting
- Start seeds indoors in late April or early May in peat pots so the roots won't be disturbed when planting.
- *Or* sow seeds directly into the garden once the soil has warmed up.
- Set out transplants after all danger of frost has passed.
- Water well.
- Mulch.

Watering
- Provide an inch of water each week that doesn't have that amount of rainfall.

Fertilizing
- Feed with liquid fertilizer monthly during the growing season.

Easy Tip
Though zinnias love long, hot days and tolerate some drought, the better the soil, the better the blooms.

Suggestions for Vigorous Growth
- If plants get too large for their area, cut them back in early summer—they'll quickly become bushy again.

Pest Control
- Few serious pests bother this plant.

Complementary Plants
- Use as a ground cover or to fill in places where perennials bloomed earlier in the season.
- Plant in containers and windowboxes with annuals of compatible colors.

Recommended Selections
- Each petal of 'Golden Orange' is highlighted with a lemon stripe.
- 'Tropic Snow' has pure-white flowers.
- Seed mixtures offer a range of colors— white, primrose-yellow, golden-yellow, and orange.

Gardening Basics

We often tell beginning gardeners that if they haven't moved a plant three times, it's probably not yet in the right place. We take comfort in what our friend, nurseryman Bud Heist, says: "Don't say we can't grow it, just say we don't yet know what it needs."

Before you consider the light, drainage, and exposure in your favorite garden spot, spend a little time learning about the soil, nutrients, pests, and plant diseases common in your area.

Soil

Some roots are reputed to be able to crack a house foundation or to break up a sidewalk, but roots are actually quite tender. When you put a plant in the soil, whether it is Bermuda grass or a baby oak, the roots will grow in the direction where resistance is least. Roots grow in the parts of the soil that offer moisture, oxygen, and nutrients.

Plants prefer to grow in soil that is a blend of clay, sand, and organic matter. The water and oxygen required by roots are plentiful in such an environment, and nutrients are available throughout. But few gardeners are blessed with perfect soil. The clay soil so abundant in north Georgia tends to have lots of moisture but little oxygen. The sandy soil prevalent along the coast has lots of oxygen but holds little water and few nutrients. The quickest way to make your soil better is to add more nutrients in the form of compost or other organic matter.

Organic Matter

Organic matter is found in manure, compost, and other materials. Ground pine bark is a common soil amendment found throughout the state of Georgia. Gardeners in the southern part of the state use ground peanut hulls. Peat moss is readily available, but it doesn't seem to persist in our soil as long as the coarser materials do. You may purchase your organic soil amendments, but if you learn how to produce them from good compost or if you find a good source of manure, you can have an unlimited free supply of organic matter.

Compost

Ever wonder why good gardeners wax eloquent about manure and compost? It's because either element, when added to a garden, can double the size and vigor of the plants. Some gardeners swear they achieve triple success when they add one of these materials to their ordinary soil. You might say that successful gardeners don't have green thumbs, they have black thumbs...from all of the manure and compost they've handled!

The reason compost is superior to any other source of organic matter is that it is *alive*. Compost is the decomposed remains of leaves, lawn clippings, pruned branches, and discarded stalks. The billions of fungi, bacteria, and other living creatures in compost are important parts of any healthy soil. Unfortunately, if you are gardening in a spot that is hard and bare, the soil has very little life in it. Plants growing in hard soil can be made beautiful, but they require more fertilizer and water to keep them looking their best.

Compost is the lazy gardener's friend. It contains billions of living creatures that help roots absorb water and nutrients. These tiny gardeners can take over some of the tasks of fertilizing and watering your plants.

Making compost never has to be complicated. Mother Nature has been composting for millions of years, and she never used a pitchfork or compost bin or expensive compost starter. Some gardeners choose to compost on a large scale, lugging bags of their neighbors' leaves up the street to dump on their compost piles. Others just throw their own leaves and clippings onto a pile and let nature take its course. Either method is fine. But the forming of compost does take time. It takes approximately six months and a thirty-gallon bag of yard trimmings to manufacture one cubic foot of compost. Mixing and turning a compost pile once a month can make the process go a bit faster.

While it's easy to make compost, it might be even easier to buy soil amendments at a garden center. But how much of this supplemental material does one need to make a difference in the soil? Dr. Tim Smalley, Professor of Horticulture at the University of Georgia, recommends spreading a layer of compost two inches thick over a garden flower bed and then mixing it with the soil underneath. In practical terms, that's two cubic feet of soil conditioner for every eight square feet of flower bed. You can see why composters are caught "borrowing" their neighbors' leaves at night!

The organic matter should be mixed to a depth of six to eight inches in the soil. With the addition of organic matter the soil will loosen, and it will stay loose for years. Oxygen will penetrate to where the roots are growing. The organic matter will absorb excess water and hold it in reserve for the plant to use when drier times come.

Watering

It seems simple enough to water an outdoor plant, but most gardeners either over-water or under-water their plants. Proper watering is accomplished differently in different parts of the state. Sandy soil drains so well that water must be applied twice a week during a blistering summer. Clay soil holds too much water. Plants in clay soil must be watered less often, or they will succumb to root rot.

The amount of water to use also differs among plants. A shallow-rooted fern might need one-fourth gallon of water applied every other day. A densely rooted lawn requires six hundred gallons per thousand square feet every week. A new tree might require three gallons twice a week for one month and afterwards only need watering when a drought occurs.

Your own observations are best when you are determining when and how much to water. Here are some tips to get you started:

- Water container plants until the water runs out the bottom.
- Do not water again until the top inch of soil is dry.
- Put a hose at the base of a newly installed plant and thoroughly soak the root ball once a week. As the plant begins to grow larger, take into consideration that the size of the root zone will also increase.
- Use shallow cans to measure the amount of water applied by your lawn sprinkler. Put six cans in the area being sprinkled and run the system for an hour. Then measure the depth of water in all of the cans. If the average depth of water is one-half inch, you will know the grass root zone has been irrigated. This may take one to two hours.
- If summer restrictions limit your watering, determine which plants would cost the most to replace, and water them first. It makes more sense to save a specimen maple tree than to keep ten dollars worth of petunias alive.
- An inexpensive water timer and a few soaker hoses can be a gardener's best friends.

Mulch

If a plant's roots are subjected to a long Georgia drought, even the toughest plant in the finest soil will suffer. Mulching will help you avoid this problem. Georgia's millions of pine trees give us two of the best mulches in the world, pine straw and pine bark chips. Mulch acts like a blanket. It keeps moisture in the soil, and it prevents plant roots from becoming too hot or too cold. Other good mulches include shredded fall leaves, wood chips, and shredded cypress bark. Few gardeners succeed without placing a one- to two-inch layer of mulch on top of the soil around all of their plants.

Nutrients

Plants need nitrogen, phosphorus, and potassium in order to grow well. When you buy a bag of fertilizer, you will see three numbers on the label. These numbers indicate the amounts of nitrogen, phosphorus, and potassium in the fertilizer. The numbers represent the percentage of each nutrient in the mixture. For example, a bag of 10-10-10 fertilizer contains 10% nitrogen (N), 10% phosphorus (P), and 10% potassium (K). The other 70% is just clay.

Each nutrient serves a function in the overall good health of a plant. So how do you know which fertilizer to buy when your garden center offers dozens of combinations of the three nutrient numbers? Just look at the numbers on the bag and remember: Up, Down, and All Around.

Up: Nitrogen promotes leaf growth. That's why lawn fertilizer has a high nitrogen percentage. A common turf fertilizer is a 16-4-8, but some brands have even more nitrogen than this. Grass leaves are mowed off constantly, so nitrogen is needed to help grow more of them.

Down: Phosphorus is important in the formation of roots and is very important for flower, seed, and fruit growth. That's why so-called "starter fertilizers" and "bloom fertilizers" have high percentages of phosphorus.

All Around: Potassium increases overall cell health. When your plant is under stress from drought or from cold, adequate potassium helps the plant withstand the crisis. "Winterizer" fertilizer for lawns is a good choice for grass that must endure such conditions. Its potassium percentage is high to help the grass fight winter cold damage.

It is not necessary to buy a different fertilizer for each of the plant types you have in your landscape. You really can't hurt a plant by applying the wrong fertilizer. Your perennials won't be damaged by the application of "azalea fertilizer." The lawn won't be hurt if you fertilize it with 10-10-10. There may be some situations in which one type of fertilizer is marginally better; for example, a "slow-release turf fertilizer" might be especially desirable for some types of grass. But you can do quite well with the purchase of just three main types of fertilizer: 16-4-8 for your lawn, 6-12-12 for new plants, and 10-10-10 for everything else.

How do you know what amount of fertilizer to apply? How much nutrition does your soil already hold? Do you need any lime? To find out, you need to perform a soil test.

Soil Test

There are two ways to test your soil. You can purchase an inexpensive gardener's test kit with simple chemicals and test tubes and do it yourself, or you can take some of your soil to your local county Extension Service office for a low-cost analysis.

Test kits are economical and simple to use. To use one, you'll mix your soil with water, then add a few drops of indicator chemical that will cause the water to change color. If you feel confident that you can match the color of the water with the colors on the small color wheel that is provided, you can determine which nutrients you need to add to your soil. If you don't trust your powers of analysis, you might want to compare your conclusions with those of the University of Georgia Soil Testing Laboratory through your local county Extension Service office.

Having soil tested by the Extension Service is a simple process as well. Collect several scoops of dirt from different areas of your yard and mix them together. The Extension Service needs just one cup of this soil mixture for the test. Put the soil in a bag, take it to your local Extension office, and tell the Extension agent what you intend to grow in it. The soil will be shipped to a laboratory in Athens. Within ten days you will receive a mailed report describing the nutrients present in your soil, the amounts in which they are present, and specific recommendations for correct fertilizer use.

Lime

Though lime does not offer plant nutrients (aside from calcium, which plants need in small amounts), it helps plants absorb nutrients more efficiently. Georgia soils, particularly in the northern half of the state, tend to be acidic. In an acidic soil, plant roots can't collect the nitrogen, phosphorus, and potassium they need to function. Lime makes soil less acidic. Soil acidity is measured in numbers from 1 to 14 on what is called the pH scale. Most plants prefer soil that has a pH of 6.0 to 6.5. A hard clay subsoil may have a pH of 4.5. It takes a lot of lime to move the pH up to 6.5. Your soil test will determine the pH of your soil and the amount of lime it needs.

Pests and Diseases

The same conditions that make our gardens so beautiful make Georgia a happy homeland for insect and disease pests. A long growing season means that insect populations have time to explode each year. Our high humidity and warm temperatures are perfect for the growth of fungi and bacteria.

It cannot be said often enough that a healthy plant is the best defense against pests. A plant that grows vigorously can quickly overcome insect damage. A plant that is not stressed by its environment can resist disease spores. Many of the plants included in this book were chosen because of their strong resistance to insects and diseases. If you follow our recommendations about the proper placement of your plants and how to care for them, your garden will rarely need pesticides. If you choose the plant varieties we recommend, you will have genetic allies in your fight against pests.

Organic vs. Inorganic Gardening

If you find pests attacking your plants, what should you do? Is the problem bad enough to use a pesticide? Which pesticide should you use? Should you rely on synthetic chemicals or should you choose pesticides made from organic sources? These questions trouble all of us. Some gardeners prefer to use only organic pesticides. Others are more pragmatic, sometimes using synthetic pesticides, occasionally preferring organic ones, but always striving to use the smallest amounts possible in every case.

There is no single correct answer to the question: Which is best— organic or inorganic gardening? Synthetic pesticides for home gardeners have been repeatedly tested for safety by their manufacturers and by the federal government. Scientists and bureaucrats who advise us on environmental matters have declared that prudent use of approved pesticides offers fewer health risks than we would encounter if we avoided pesticides completely and endangered our food supply. Organic gardening does not always completely eliminate pesticide use, as it sometimes calls for the use of pesticides that come from organic sources. These organic pesticides may have risks higher or lower than synthetic ones. Fortunately, new gardening products with fewer risks appear on the market every year.

The choice between an "organic" or an "inorganic" garden is yours alone to make. You must decide whether the convenience of using synthetic pesticides offsets the hard work and constant vigilance required to completely eliminate their use.

Information on Pesticide Use

If you need advice on which pesticides to use, the best resource for assistance is the local office of the University of Georgia Cooperative Extension Service. The agents there maintain the latest research data on the most effective and least potentially harmful pesticides to use. Ask them to tell you about all of the alternatives for solving your pest problem. Then you can use your experience and wisdom to make the choices that are best for your situation.

The Name Game

Gardeners may wonder why they need to know the scientific names of plants. The answer is simple: you want to make sure the rose you purchase for your own garden is the same sweet-smelling rose you admired (and coveted) in your neighbor's garden. It's true that scientific names, which are derived from Latin or Greek, can be long and hard to pronounce. But unlike a common plant name, which often is applied to two very different plants, a scientific designation is specific and unique.

Throughout this book we identify plants by both their scientific and common names. A plant's scientific name consists of the genus (the first word) and an epithet. For example, all maples belong to the genus Acer. The epithet (in our example, rubrum) identifies a specific kind of maple. *Acer rubrum* is a red maple. The genus and epithet are always italicized and the genus name begins with a capital letter, while the entire epithet is always written in lower case.

A third word in the name may refer to a special variety of the plant, called a cultivar. The cultivar name is important because it designates a superior selection known for bigger blooms, better foliage, or some other noteworthy characteristic. A cultivar name is distinguished by the use of single quotation marks, as in the name Acer rubrum 'October Glory', a red maple with excellent fall leaf color. Most cultivars must be propagated by division or cuttings because they may not come true from seed.

A scientific name can change, but this happens only rarely, and there are certain rigid rules that apply to the practice of plant nomenclature. It is much easier to track down a wonderful plant if you know the full scientific name. Armed with a knowledge of both scientific and common names, you should be able to acquire the best plants for your Georgia garden.

Propagation

Once you become excited about gardening, you may develop "plant lust." You'll start to think that you must buy every new and exciting plant you discover. A much less expensive way to acquire your plants is to propagate them using seeds, cuttings, or divisions.

Growing annuals from seed works well, but it is usually the slowest method for propagating perennials and is not always successful. The good news is that once they are well established in your garden, many perennial plants can be easily divided and transplanted, providing a constant supply of new plants.

When dividing a perennial, dig up the entire plant and separate it into pieces. You may dig up a mature clump and use a digging fork and your fingers to tease apart the roots, or you can make a clean cut with a straight-edged shovel to divide the large clump into smaller pieces. Make sure each piece has roots and buds. Remember, always have the new garden area prepared ahead of time for the new divisions, and don't let the roots dry out. Once all the divisions are planted, water them well. They'll grow large in no time!

Rooting stem cuttings is another option for propagating both perennials and annuals, as well as many shrubs. The important point to remember about cuttings is to take cuttings during the correct season. Timing is more important with shrubs than with perennials and annuals. Rooting stem cuttings provides a simple means to overwinter a piece of an annual that has grown too big to save in its present size; thus, it can be preserved and propagated again.

Another easy method for propagating plants, including most azaleas and hydrangeas, is layering. Penny McHenry, president of the American Hydrangea Society and a keen Atlanta gardener, propagates some of her favorite hydrangeas by bending young branches so they touch the ground. Making sure to loosen the dirt at the point of contact, she places soil and organic matter on top of the stem and uses a brick to weigh it down. Within two months, Penny has a newly rooted plant that can be cut off from the main plant and transplanted to a new location.

These are just a few suggestions for ways to get more out of your garden or to share your bounty with friends. Some of the most wonderful gardens started with "a piece of this and a division of that." Who knows, you may develop your own favorite technique for propagating a special rose or that mildew-resistant phlox you discover in your garden!

With these few tips you now have an overview of the basic information needed to become a gardener. To obtain the truly valuable skills of gardening, you will have to practice the 4-H Club motto: Learn by Doing. You will have to don your old jeans, take up your shovel, and dig!

If you keep your heart and mind open to the nuances of nature, you will cultivate more than just pretty flowers and strong trees. Both your plants and you yourself will grow in your beautiful garden. Fayetteville nurseryman Steven Stinchcomb may have said it best: "Some people are just gardeners in their heads and some people become gardeners in their hearts."

Good Gardening!

Glossary

Alkaline soil: soil with a pH greater than 7.0. It lacks acidity, often because it has limestone in it.

All-purpose fertilizer: powdered, liquid, or granular fertilizer with a balanced proportion of the three key nutrients—nitrogen (N), phosphorus (P), and potassium (K). It is suitable for maintenance nutrition for most plants.

Annual: a plant that lives its entire life in one season. It is genetically determined to germinate, grow, flower, set seed, and die the same year.

Balled and burlapped: describes a tree or shrub grown in the field whose soilball was wrapped with protective burlap and twine when the plant was dug up to be sold or transplanted.

Bare root: describes plants that have been packaged without any soil around their roots. (Often young shrubs and trees purchased through the mail arrive with their exposed roots covered with moist peat or sphagnum moss, sawdust, or similar material, and wrapped in plastic.)

Barrier plant: a plant that has intimidating thorns or spines and is sited purposely to block foot traffic or other access to the home or yard.

Beneficial insects: insects or their larvae that prey on pest organisms and their eggs. They may be flying insects, such as ladybugs, parasitic wasps, praying mantids, and soldier bugs, or soil dwellers such as predatory nematodes, spiders, and ants.

Berm: a narrow, raised ring of soil around a tree, used to hold water so it will be directed to the root zone.

Bract: a modified leaf structure on a plant stem near its flower, resembling a petal. Often it is more colorful and visible than the actual flower, as in dogwood.

Bud union: the place where the top of a plant was grafted to the rootstock; usually refers to roses.

Canopy: the overhead branching area of a tree, usually referring to its extent including foliage.

Cold hardiness: the ability of a perennial plant to survive the winter cold in a particular area.

Composite: a flower that is actually composed of many tiny flowers. Typically, they are flat clusters of tiny, tight florets, sometimes surrounded by wider-petaled florets. Composite flowers are highly attractive to bees and beneficial insects.

Compost: organic matter that has undergone progressive decomposition by microbial and macrobial activity until it is reduced to a spongy, fluffy texture. Added to soil of any type, it improves the soil's ability to hold air and water and to drain well.

Corm: the swollen energy-storing structure, analogous to a bulb, under the soil at the base of the stem of plants such as crocus and gladiolus.

119

Crown: the base of a plant at, or just beneath, the surface of the soil where the roots meet the stems.

Cultivar: a CULTIvated VARiety. It is a naturally occurring form of a plant that has been identified as special or superior and is purposely selected for propagation and production.

Deadhead: a pruning technique that removes faded flower heads from plants to improve their appearances, abort seed production, and stimulate further flowering.

Deciduous plants: unlike evergreens, these trees and shrubs lose their leaves in the fall.

Desiccation: drying out of foliage tissues, usually due to drought or wind.

Division: the practice of splitting apart perennial plants to create several smaller-rooted segments. The practice is useful for controlling the plant's size and for acquiring more plants; it is also essential to the health and continued flowering of certain ones.

Dormancy: the period, usually the winter, when perennial plants temporarily cease active growth and rest. Dormant is the verb form, as used in this sentence: *Some plants, like spring-blooming bulbs, go dormant in the summer.*

Established: the point at which a newly planted tree, shrub, or flower begins to produce new growth, either foliage or stems. This is an indication that the roots have recovered from transplant shock and have begun to grow and spread.

Evergreen: perennial plants that do not lose their foliage annually with the onset of winter. Needled or broadleaf foliage will persist and continues to function on a plant through one or more winters, aging and dropping unobtrusively in cycles of three or four years or more.

Floret: a tiny flower, usually one of many forming a cluster, that comprises a single blossom.

Foliar: of or about foliage—usually refers to the practice of spraying foliage, as in fertilizing or treating with insecticide; leaf tissues absorb liquid directly for fast results, and the soil is not affected.

Germinate: to sprout. Germination is a fertile seed's first stage of development.

Graft (union): the point on the stem of a woody plant with sturdier roots where a stem from a highly ornamental plant is inserted so that it will join with it. Roses are commonly grafted.

Hardscape: the permanent, structural, nonplant part of a landscape, such as walls, sheds, pools, patios, arbors, and walkways.

Herbaceous: plants having fleshy or soft stems that die back with frost; the opposite of woody.

Hybrid: a plant that is the result of intentional or natural cross-pollination between two or more plants of the same species or genus.

Low water demand: describes plants that tolerate dry soil for varying periods of time. Typically, they have succulent, hairy, or silvery-gray foliage and tuberous roots or taproots.

Mulch: a layer of material over bare soil to protect it from erosion and compaction by rain, and to discourage weeds. It may be inorganic (gravel, fabric) or organic (wood chips, bark, pine needles, chopped leaves).

Naturalize: (*a*) to plant seeds, bulbs, or plants in a random, informal pattern as they would appear in their natural habitats; (*b*) to adapt to and spread throughout adopted habitats (a tendency of some nonnative plants).

Nectar: the sweet fluid produced by glands on flowers that attract pollinators such as hummingbirds and honeybees, for whom it is a source of energy.

Organic material, organic matter: any material or debris that is derived from plants. It is carbon-based material capable of undergoing decomposition and decay.

Peat moss: organic matter from peat sedges (United States) or sphagnum mosses (Canada), often used to improve soil texture. The acidity of sphagnum peat moss makes it ideal for boosting or maintaining soil acidity while also improving its drainage.

Perennial: a flowering plant that lives over two or more seasons. Many die back with frost, but their roots survive the winter and generate new shoots in the spring.

pH: a measurement of the relative acidity (low pH) or alkalinity (high pH) of soil or water based on a scale of 1 to 14, 7 being neutral. Individual plants require soil to be within a certain range so that nutrients can dissolve in moisture and be available to them.

Pinch: to remove tender stems and/or leaves by pressing them between thumb and forefinger. This pruning technique encourages branching, compactness, and flowering in plants, or it removes aphids clustered at growing tips.

Pollen: the yellow, powdery grains in the center of a flower. A plant's male sex cells, they are transferred to the female plant parts by means of wind or animal pollinators to fertilize them and create seeds.

Raceme: an arrangement of single-stalked flowers along an elongated, unbranched axis.

Rhizome: a swollen energy-storing stem structure, similar to a bulb, that lies horizontally in the soil, with roots emerging from its lower surface and growth shoots from a growing point at or near its tip, as in bearded iris.

Rootbound (or potbound): the condition of a plant that has been confined in a container too long, its roots having been forced to wrap around themselves and even swell out of the container. Successful transplanting or repotting requires untangling and trimming away of some of the matted roots.

Root flare: the transition at the base of a tree trunk where the bark tissue begins to differentiate and roots begin to form just before entering the soil. This area should not be covered with soil when planting a tree.

Self-seeding: the tendency of some plants to sow their seeds freely around the yard. It creates many seedlings the following season that may or may not be welcome.

Semievergreen: tending to be evergreen in a mild climate but deciduous in a rigorous one.

Shearing: the pruning technique whereby plant stems and branches are cut uniformly with long-bladed pruning shears (hedge shears) or powered hedge trimmers. It is used when creating and maintaining hedges and topiary.

Slow-acting fertilizer: fertilizer that is water insoluble and therefore releases its nutrients gradually as a function of soil temperature, moisture, and related microbial activity. Typically granular, it may be organic or synthetic.

Succulent growth: the sometimes undesirable production of fleshy, water-storing leaves or stems that results from overfertilization.

Sucker: a new-growing shoot. Underground plant roots produce suckers to form new stems and spread by means of these suckering roots to form large plantings, or colonies. Some plants produce root suckers or branch suckers as a result of pruning or wounding.

Tuber: a type of underground storage structure in a plant stem, analogous to a bulb. It generates roots below and stems above ground (example: dahlia).

Variegated: having various colors or color patterns. The term usually refers to plant foliage that is streaked, edged, blotched, or mottled with a contrasting color—often green with yellow, cream, or white.

White grubs: fat, off-white, wormlike larvae of Japanese beetles. They reside in the soil and feed on plant (especially grass) roots until summer when they emerge as beetles to feed on plant foliage.

Wings: (*a*) the corky tissue that forms edges along the twigs of some woody plants such as winged euonymus; (*b*) the flat, dried extension of tissue on some seeds, such as maple, that catch the wind and help them disseminate.

Bibliography

Armitage, Allan. 1989. *Herbaceous Perennial Plants: A Treatise on Their Culture and Garden Attributes*. Varsity Press, Inc. Athens, GA.

Bender, Steven and Felder Rushing. 1993. *Passalong Plants*. The University of North Carolina Press. Chapel Hill, NC.

Brooklyn Botanic Garden. *Plants and Gardens Handbooks*, many different subjects. List available from Brooklyn Botanic Garden, 1000 Washington Ave., Brooklyn, NY.

Burke, Ken (ed.). 1980. *Shrubs and Hedges*. The American Horticultural Society. Franklin Center, PA.

Burke, Ken (ed.). 1982. *Gardening in the Shade*. The American Horticultural Society, Franklin Center, PA.

Dirr, Michael. 1990. *Manual of Woody Landscape Plants*. Stipes Publishing. Champaign, IL.

Gardiner, J.M. 1989. *Magnolias*. Globe Pequot Press, Chester, PA.

Gates, Galen et al. 1994. *Shrubs and Vines*. Pantheon Books. New York, NY.

Greenlee, John. 1992. *The Encyclopedia of Ornamental Grasses*. Rodale Press. Emmaus, PA.

Halfacre, R. Gordon and Anne R. Shawcroft. 1979. *Landscape Plants of the Southeast*. Sparks Press. Raleigh, NC.

Harper, Pamela and Frederick McGourty. 1985. *Perennials: How to Select, Grow and Enjoy*. HP Books. Tucson, AZ.

Heath, Brent and Becky. 1995. *Daffodils for American Gardens*. Elliott & Clark Publishing. Washington, DC.

Hipps, Carol Bishop. 1994. *In a Southern Garden*. Macmillan Publishing. New York, NY.

Lawrence, Elizabeth. 1991. *A Southern Garden*. The University of North Carolina Press. Chapel Hill, NC.

Lawson-Hall, Toni and Brian Rothera. 1996. *Hydrangeas*. Timber Press. Portland, OR.

Loewer, Peter. 1992. *Tough Plants for Tough Places*. Rodale Press. Emmaus, PA.

Mikel, John. 1994. *Ferns for American Gardens*. Macmillan Publishing. New York, NY.

Ogden, Scott. 1994. *Garden Bulbs for the South*. Taylor Publishing. Dallas, TX.

Still, Steven. 1994. *Manual of Herbaceous Ornamental Plants*. 4th edition. Stipes Publishing. Champaign, IL.

Vengris, Jonas and William A. Torello. 1982. *Lawns*. Thomson Publications. Fresno, CA.

Winterrowd, Wayne. 1992. *Annuals for Connoisseurs*. Prentice Hall. New York, NY.

Photography Credits

Thomas Eltzroth: pages 11, 12, 16, 24, 26, 28, 40, 42, 44, 46, 52, 58, 60, 68, 76, 80, 82, 88, 90, 96, 100, 104, 108, 110

Jerry Pavia: pages 9, 10, 28, 32, 38, 50, 62, 64, 66, 78, 84, 86, 98, 102, 106

Liz Ball and Rick Ray: pages 34, 36, 70, 72, 94

William Adams: pages 18, 54

Erica Glasener: pages 14, 56

Pam Harper: pages 22, 48

Andre Viette: pages 8, 20

Carol Reese: page 74

Felder Rushing: page 92

Plant Index

Want to know more about Georgia gardening?

Interested in terrific trees for Georgia? Do you want healthful and tasty herbs, fruits, and vegetables from your Georgia garden? How about stunning Georgia shrubs?

If you enjoy *50 Great Flowers for Georgia*, you will appreciate similar books featuring Georgia trees, vegetables (including fruits and herbs), and shrubs. These valuable books also deserve a place in your gardening library.

50 Great Trees for Georgia

Erica Glasener and Walter Reeves recommend fifty great trees for Georgia. They offer fantastic options on small flowering trees, great evergreens, and trees that delight with multiseason interest.

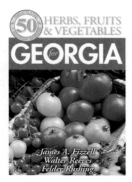

50 Great Herbs, Fruits and Vegetables for Georgia

If you are inclined to "edibles" in your Georgia garden, this is the book for you. It provides valuable advice on how to select, plant and grow tasty herbs, luscious fruits, and flavorful vegetables. Written by James A. Fizzell, Walter Reeves, and Felder Rushing, this book offers more than seventy-five years of gardening wisdom all in an easy to-use-format.

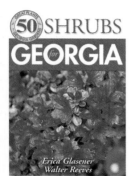

50 Great Shrubs for Georgia

If you want guidance on great shrubs for Georgia, this is the book for you. From the boxwood to the flowering azalea, Erica Glasener and Walter Reeves share their gardening insight on fifty wonderful shrubs for Georgia.

Look for each of these books today.